T0114929

JAKEB BROCK

The New Consciousness

What Our World Needs Most

BALBOA.PRESS

A DIVISION OF HAY HOUSE

Balboa Press books may be ordered through booksellers or by contacting:

Balboa Press
A Division of Hay House
1663 Liberty Drive
Bloomington, IN 47403
www.balboapress.com
844-682-1282

Because of the dynamic nature of the Internet, any web addresses or links contained in this book may have changed since publication and may no longer be valid. The views expressed in this work are solely those of the author and do not necessarily reflect the views of the publisher, and the publisher hereby disclaims any responsibility for them.

The author of this book does not dispense medical advice or prescribe the use of any technique as a form of treatment for physical, emotional, or medical problems without the advice of a physician, either directly or indirectly. The intent of the author is only to offer information of a general nature to help you in your quest for emotional and spiritual well-being. In the event you use any of the information in this book for yourself, which is your constitutional right, the author and the publisher assume no responsibility for your actions.

Any people depicted in stock imagery provided by Getty Images are models, and such images are being used for illustrative purposes only. Certain stock imagery © Getty Images.

Scripture taken from the Holy Bible, NEW INTERNATIONAL VERSION®. Copyright © 1973, 1978, 1984, 2011 by Biblica, Inc. All rights reserved worldwide. Used by permission. NEW INTERNATIONAL VERSION® and NIV® are registered trademarks of Biblica, Inc. Use of either trademark for the offering of goods or services requires the prior written consent of Biblica US, Inc.

Print information available on the last page.

ISBN: 978-1-9822-0808-0 (sc)
ISBN: 978-1-9822-0810-3 (hc)
ISBN: 978-1-9822-0809-7 (e)

Library of Congress Control Number: 2018908000

Balboa Press rev. date: 01/12/2021

Table of Contents

Preface

Jesus was a man, and it has been a grave mistake for us to build a world religion based on the teaching that he was God. For, by worshipping him as God, we have greatly reduced the scope to which universal man can evolve. By setting Jesus apart as a God-man, we render all of his wonderful deeds and sayings as exclusively divine and rob ourselves of the vision of ever being able to share in his experience. Essentially, we lock ourselves out of heaven forever.

Individual correction of this grave mistake is the true salvation that awaits us. The moment we realize that Jesus was the *Way Shower* and not the exclusive, one and only divine Way is the moment we are set free to embark upon the path of true spiritual enlightenment. The moment we understand that when Jesus said, "I and the Father are one," (John 10:30) he was not speaking of himself only but rather potentially of every human being that has ever and will ever live on this planet is the moment that the age-old dream of Adamic consciousness is shattered.

Jesus' giftedness and power had their source in his state of consciousness—a consciousness expressive of the full revelation of man's potential for being reconciled to and united with God. He never intended that this highly evolved state of consciousness be construed as exclusive and belonging only to him. In fact, this *Christ consciousness*, while perfected by the man Jesus, has been attained by numerous others throughout this age of Adam. These others have come from different lands across the globe. Like Jesus, their lives were primarily testimonies of the power and presence of God—a power and presence that transforms any and every individual human experience it touches. Thus the signs and wonders that Jesus performed as the validating proof that this state of consciousness was God-union realized were also performed by the others. And the teaching of these masters was also of one accord. What is this teaching? Precisely that the state of consciousness that they were moving in is attainable for all men and women. It is, in fact, our ultimate evolutionary destiny as a species.

What all this implies is that it is not enough for us to worship Jesus as God and thereby hope to receive some sort of vicarious spiritual endowment. We must become like him and attain the state of consciousness that was his for ourselves. This is our true salvation and collective destiny. And it is within the reach of every man, woman, and child on this planet, regardless of any human distinction, such as race, skin color, language, culture, etc. *If we have the breath of life as a human being, we can attain Christ consciousness.*

Once we have gained the revelation of this amazing spiritual truth, the question then becomes: how? Developing spiritual consciousness is not like acquiring knowledge. You cannot learn it in a university. It is a *transformational experience* that only comes to us as we are exposed to the truth. Thus all we can do is to avail ourselves to God's Spirit and hope that the truth inherent in scripture and other wisdom teachings gains a solid foothold in our consciousness.

To attain the revelation of our true destiny of oneness with God—both as individuals and as a species—sets us free from the dualistic materialistic Adamic consciousness that has dominated human experience for at least the past six thousand years. This darkened consciousness has been the cause of every malignant aspect of human life—the strife, discord, war, disease, poverty, and death. Adamic consciousness has built the world that we have inherited. And who can deny that it is a world rife with suffering and misery?

Consciousness produces outward conditions according to its kind. This means that there can be no true and lasting change for the better in our world until there has been a true and lasting change in the collective consciousness. Therefore though our attempts at healing our world symptomatically may be well intended, they are inherently misdirected. When we try to patch up the outer picture without tending to the necessary inward transformation, we put the cart before the horse. Whereas, if we would see to the evolvement of our collective consciousness as a top priority, all the outward changes we have been yearning for would follow of their own accord. Jesus gave credence to this truth, when he said, "Seek ye first the Kingdom of God, and all these things will be added to you." (Matthew 6:33). To seek the Kingdom of God first is to focus our attention primarily on the realm of spiritual consciousness within us. This is really all that is required of us.

While the consciousness of God union is by no means new in the purely existential sense, its appropriation in the collective human experience would not only be new; it would be revolutionary. And yet, it is my firm conviction that this is the threshold upon which we currently stand. Despite appearances to the contrary, mankind is finally ready to climb to the next rung on the ladder of spiritual evolution. We are ready at long last to finish with the Adam dream—the age-old dualistic dream of the knowledge of good and evil—and wake up to the reality of *one God, one good*. For six thousand years we have been a race of prodigals. We have justified this anti-God stance to the degree that we have completely lost sight of the true reality. We have even put forth the idea that the Adam mind is a highly advanced evolutionary state. But all this has been nothing but a grand deception. Why did we willingly embrace such an obvious deception? Plainly and simply: we were not ready for the truth.

All our wars, strife, hatred, and fear have had their source in the Adam mind, because consciousness *must reflect outwardly* as attitudes and conditions. In the same way, the new consciousness, once fully appropriated in the collective psyche, will bring unparalleled peace, harmony, and healing to the human scene.

This was Jesus' vision for how to effect lasting change. He knew that a new societal order that was the product of force or imposition would not endure. He knew that there had to first be a change in the collective consciousness. So he did not attempt to establish a socio-political realignment (in sharp contrast to worldly kings and emperors). Rather he took on the humble role of an itinerant spiritual teacher, teaching truth in language that even a child could understand. Why? Because this is how consciousness begins to grow. Jesus' simplistic teachings were the seeds for the collective consciousness evolution we are only now beginning to witness. Looking back therefore, there can be no doubt of the efficacy of such a methodology.

So it is that what we are witnessing in our time is in actuality the fruition of the Gospel of Christ—not of organized religion, which has often become hopelessly sidetracked with false teachings—but of the pure essence of the Gospel. True, it has taken two thousand years, but Jesus never put forth a timetable. Rather he gave us the full teaching, made certain it would be preserved for future generations, and washed his hands of the outcome.

In this sense Jesus became the guardian and primary proponent for the new consciousness, in that first he demonstrated it in his own life and second passed it down through a chain of apostolic commission. But he was not the first to discover this consciousness. Many enlightened individuals preceded him in the historical framework of this age of man. Ancient Indian sages codified the science of yoga long before Jesus was born, so that in that land the light of the new consciousness has been shining since time immemorial. And we must not forget the early Hebrews that gave us the Old Testament writings. Though their teachings were often veiled, they were nonetheless full of truth. They gave Adam his name and symbolic generic persona; they brought to light the nuances of Adam's dualistic state of consciousness, and they were the ones who imparted to us the knowledge that consciousness is not only responsible for outer conditions but it also is passed down from generation to generation. In other words, they were the ones who predicted that the so-called Adamic consciousness would produce a world exactly like the one we now live in.

In light of this historical evidence that the new consciousness has in fact been known to mystics since the beginning of the age, we can now fully appreciate the efforts of such seers and understand the nature of true human greatness and altruism. These have been the true servants of mankind. And Jesus became the greatest servant of all by being willing to die on a Roman cross, so that the new consciousness might win out in the end.

The idea that there will be two advents of the Christ Spirit on earth has been the subject of much speculation. The man Jesus was of course the first advent, but the second advent will not be a man; it will be the birth of the new consciousness in the collective psyche. And as Jesus humbly taught, this glorious and enduring appearance of the Christ will far outshine the first advent, wherein only the hidden seeds of glory were planted.

Part One

The Rise of the New
Consciousness in
Western Civilization

Chapter One

The Human Psyche

We are human beings. But what exactly does being human entail? What is our essential makeup?

Many have undertaken to answer these questions through the knowledge gained from scientific empirical process. Others have pondered and arrived at answers through philosophical conjecture. Still others have studied the teachings of religious and spiritual masters. But the answers we are really seeking—the only answers that will satisfy us—are those that transcend these exclusive temporal processes and show themselves to be timeless and universal. In other words, what we are really yearning to know as we answer these questions is *the truth*.

What is truth? Sadly, our modern view of truth is that of a skeptic. And our skepticism is neither innocent nor naïve. Rather it is highly sophisticated, having been born in the incubator of thousands of years of power politics and arrogance. Thus the prevailing attitude about truth is first, that it cannot be found in simplistic religious teachings, and second, that it is an adaptable concept, which can change colors like a chameleon in order to suit a certain mood or fancy. This has given impetus to the school of thought that truth as an absolute does not exist and therefore can never be delineated as such. It is rather a relative concept that pertains primarily to matters of expediency.

The foremost spokesperson for this modern version of truth was a man who had no idea that that was what he was doing or that he would be long remembered as such. He simply voiced the prevailing attitude when speaking to one for whom truth was both known and absolute. This was, of course, the Roman Governor Pontius Pilate who played the unenviable role of being the legal authority to decree that Jesus be crucified. His cynical response to Jesus' claim that he came into the world to testify to truth has echoed down throughout the age as a kind of skeptic's motto. "What is truth?" he asked, mockingly. (John 18:38). Three simple words uttered off-the-cuff by a man admittedly in the grip of self-glorification and expediency. What is truth? It is whatever I, Pontius Pilate, say it is. And what is my authority for making my own truth? It is my political power—a power that has put me in the position of being the one to crucify the Christ.

Thus what we see in this well documented enactment between a high Roman dignitary and a dusty itinerant Hebrew spiritual teacher are in actuality the only two possibilities by which truth can be known. It can either be the arbitrary changeable tool of socio-political expediency as expressed by Pilate and embraced by the entire secular world of men or it can be the absolute reality about which Jesus came to testify.

The world has chosen its spokesperson in these matters. Pontius Pilate represents not only political authority but also wealth, influence, manipulation, propaganda, mind control and all other forms of human power. The truth as wielded by these human demagogues has been used not to liberate and enlighten the masses but rather to oppress and subjugate them. Jesus' truth on the other hand, was put forth in order that we might be set free from the inner bondage to ignorance and fear. So accepting the fact that absolute truth really does exist, we can then set about the task of answering the questions about man and God that have riddled our species since time immemorial.

Indeed knowing the truth can be a great liberating power in our individual lives, but it is not our ultimate goal. Our ultimate goal is the development of spiritual consciousness—the raising of consciousness, both individually and collectively, out of its current degradation and bondage to fear, duality, and prodigality and into the light of the perfection-of-being found in realized union with God. Jesus taught the importance of knowing the truth because he knew that it was through the attaining of this knowledge that consciousness stirs and expands to new growth.

Every individual human being has an inward essence or self that the spiritual masters of our race have most often referred to as *consciousness*. This essence of our individual being constitutes our core identity, after all other lesser defining human functions, such as ego, intellect, emotional makeup, and physicality are stripped away. Thus there is a phenomenon of individual consciousness to recognize and seek to gain understanding about, and there is also the phenomenon of a collective or race consciousness.

The fact that there are these two separate phenomena pertaining to human consciousness is no great mystery. The collective consciousness of man is simply the reflection of the dominant individual consciousness operating in any given setting and timeframe. For example, theoretically the collective consciousness in California in the year A.D. 2000 would be different than the collective consciousness in Greece in the year 300 B.C. But theory aside, since consciousness is not a matter of mere culture, fads, or opinions, but rather is spiritually based and activated, it tends to be remarkably consistent. Somewhat like biological genetic inheritance, consciousness is often passed down from generation to generation and subliminally transmitted in the individual psyche at conception. This is because the race consciousness has been fiercely adhered to by each successive generation and promoted as a reality belief system. So it is that we have individual consciousness impacting collective consciousness and collective consciousness impacting individual consciousness. Like a revolving door, human consciousness gets passed into and out of all manifestations of the human psyche.

If consciousness is not a matter of cultural assimilation or diversity, what is it? What does it mean to say that consciousness is spiritual? One thing that we can deduce immediately is that the cementing of consciousness is somehow connected to the prevailing belief system and reality view. This means that consciousness and truth are connected and play off of one another, though consciousness is not necessarily always grounded in truth. Rather it can just as easily be established *in opposition to* truth. The point is that in either case consciousness and truth are interrelated. Now truth, when it is the real deal, is a spiritual dynamic. This means that it has a creative capacity, which in turn empowers consciousness with this same endowment. Therefore consciousness becomes a creative force in its own right. It does not matter whether consciousness is grounded in truth or in opposition to truth. Its relation to and interaction with truth has made consciousness a creator. The importance of this principle is that recognizing the character of our state of consciousness can then become a key to understanding why our outward conditions are as they are. If consciousness is in opposition to truth and therefore unenlightened, it will produce difficult problematic conditions. On the other hand, the same consciousness, when in harmony with truth, will produce benign, harmonious conditions. This holds true in both the individual and collective arenas.

Our individual consciousness creates our individual destiny and conditions, while the collective world consciousness creates the climate and conditions on a national and global scale.

The human psyche then is actually under the dominion of consciousness. The other major aspects of our psyche—ego, intellect, emotion, and physicality—may seem dominant each in their turn, but the decisive quality is that these have no creative mandate. In other words, they have no real power. Only our spiritual consciousness has this capability and function. To prove this we have only to consider the common conflicting interplay in the human psyche. For example, on any given day our intellect may feel empowered, while our emotions tell us we are sad, and our physical body screams that it is in pain. But none of this has any lasting effect on our psyche. Our consciousness remains firmly and quietly in control, dictating our true ongoing condition, while none of the fluctuations of our other faculties carry any real weight. Thus through our own experience and observation we arrive at this crucial maxim: *in order to effectuate real and lasting change in the conditions of our life situation, we must have a change of consciousness.* Without a change of consciousness we will keep on producing the same results, regardless of what we are thinking, feeling, or experiencing in our body.

Therefore consciousness is the true indicator of our experience in this life. It is the cause behind every effect and the inward source for every outward manifestation. And this applies to both its individual and collective aspects. Individually, consciousness governs and overrides our will, emotions, intelligence quotient, and bodily strength. It determines whether we are healthy or sickly, rich or poor, free or oppressed, etc. It even determines the kind of death we will experience. While in the collective arena, it is consciousness that determines our national alliances, quality of culture, economic disparities, etc. It determines whether there will be peace on earth or perpetual hostility and war. It determines whether there will be abundance and plenty or famine and abject poverty.

Consciousness does not fluctuate or change from day to day. On the contrary, it tends to become so entrenched in the human psyche that it takes great upheaval to change it. This explains how we came to be the recipients of Adam's consciousness and have, with the exception of a few courageous individuals, stayed stuck in that consciousness for six thousand years. And when we consider the creative power of consciousness, it is no wonder that the same conditions have consistently plagued humankind throughout this age. Even though we have undoubtedly increased in intellectual prowess and become more sophisticated in our emotional responses, not much has changed in human society since Cain murdered his brother in a jealous fit.

It is consciousness that has created the world, as we now know it. But this is not commonly known or accepted. Most people believe that our world is primarily the reflection of human effort, good intentions, and ingenuity. They cite the progressive state of our science, technology, and overall standard of living as proof that man's efforts are little by little transforming the earth into a Homo sapiens utopia. But this is really just wishful thinking. The reality is that the world of man has not changed essentially for the past six thousand years, and the reason is that there has been no change in the collective consciousness. There have been individuals who have experienced great breakthroughs in the realm of spiritual consciousness, but these have been too few and too quiet to impact the collective consciousness. In their individual lives they have witnessed the wondrous creative capacity of consciousness. They have seen their life situations become virtually problem free and fulfilled. They have watched as bodily ailments disappeared without any residual effect and seen lack and limitation give way to abundance and sufficiency. They have experienced their tentative fearful countenance being transformed through the enlightenment of the truth. But the collective entity has not paid any heed to such testimonies. Rather it has clung to its status quo mandate, despite the persistent age-long global demonstration of ignorance, suffering, hatred, violence, incurable disease, and torment over the inevitable prospect of death.

Consciousness and Evolution

Everybody accepts the fact that human beings are evolutionary creatures on some level. Even if we adamantly oppose the scientific theory that our species evolved from a lower form of primate, we generally are at least amenable to the idea that human beings have evolved socially and psychologically from a bestial evolutionary state to a more civilized one. What many people do not realize is that in accepting such a commonly held view they are actually accepting the idea that consciousness is a creative force in the human scene and that it is evolutionary by nature.

What does it mean to be evolutionary by nature? It means that consciousness, when left to itself, naturally seeks the evolutionary fulfillment for which it was created. This same dynamic can be readily witnessed in other life forms in the natural world. A tiger will naturally seek to become the full essence of what it means to be a tiger; a fish will evolve into its highest fish form; a plant will push toward the full evolutionary fulfillment of flowering or bearing fruit, etc. And in the same way our species naturally would evolve into its full created potential, if we did not thwart that evolutionary impulse.

The full evolutionary potential of man, once realized, would logically express benignity, goodness, and perfection in its outward manifestation. So why would we try to thwart such a natural evolutionary impulse? This is a complex question. Before it can be adequately addressed, we must first admit that what we are currently manifesting in the human scene is *not* our full evolutionary potential. This is necessary because one of the main hindrances to our being able to demonstrate fullness is the fact that we have as a collective unit embraced a very big lie. This lie is that man has already reached his evolutionary pinnacle and that no further evolutionary expression awaits us.

This lie has infiltrated the collective human psyche to such a degree that it has effectively stymied our evolutionary process as a species. Keep in mind that consciousness is a creative power. Therefore if we had fully evolved in truth, our world would reflect that fullness in manifestation. Disease, death, poverty, and sin would then be non-existent. But the fact that our world is still filled with misery and fear shows that the evolutionary progress of our collective consciousness has somewhere along the way been thwarted.

Now let us suppose that this one lie was exposed and rejected in the collective consciousness. What would happen? Just the removal of that one obstacle would allow us to once again give impetus to our natural evolutionary impulses. The collective consciousness would break out of its dark holding pattern and blossom like a desert rose. The great lie would give way to the truth, and human consciousness would be filled with the light and power of God.

Unfortunately, throughout this age of Adam there have been those who have worked very hard at perpetuating the lie and maintaining the status quo of fear and discord. Why? Because they believed that they had something to gain from the global climate of Darwinian strife. They found it to be personally profitable and self-enhancing. They became wealthy, powerful, and sought-after. In short, they sold the age-fulfilling evolutionary progress of man in exchange for their own pitiful profit. This is why there have always been those in our world who have gravitated toward the proactive defense of the status quo. Wherever individuals have found their personal status elevated in the midst of a global climate of inequality and instability, that climate has been aggressively perpetuated. Thus the thwarting of mankind's evolutionary fulfillment has resulted.

Lest, however, we point the finger of blame at certain well-known individuals of this sort, it must also be recognized that though individual consciousness evolution can happen according to the readiness of that individual, the collective consciousness can only evolve at the pace of its weakest member. Thus the fact that there have always been those who are eager to defend a corrupt status quo in order to pursue their own profit is actually indicative of the fact that the human race has simply not been ready to demonstrate its full evolutionary thrust up to this time. Conversely, if and when the time comes that such obstructive individual inclinations cease, that will be the sign that our ultimate collective fulfillment is upon us.

In any case, the fact that consciousness development is evolutionary means that it will take place all on its own initiative, as soon as the restraints that have been holding it back are removed. This is important to keep in mind, because it implies that we need not strive for the fulfillment of consciousness evolution. We need only open ourselves to the natural evolutionary impulse of our species and ready ourselves to be a part of the new consciousness that unfolds.

Most individuals who are ready now for man's full evolution of consciousness have found their path strewn with obstacles and impediments. They have encountered a powerful intuitive reaction of resistance and inertia emanating from the present collective socio-political arena. Thus they have learned to go underground and pursue their individual unfoldment with wisdom and tenacity. Even so, this resistant world climate has not been able to derail individual expression. Why? Because the individual impulse of consciousness evolution can no more be stopped than the sun could be stopped from rising in the morning sky. Just the fact that so many individuals have succeeded in their attempt to shift gears into the new consciousness is proof of the indomitable force of consciousness evolution. This is also the greatest reason to feel hopeful about our world. When the time is ripe, nothing—not even the greedy intent of status quo defenders—will be able to thwart the evolution of the collective consciousness and the dawn of the new age of man.

Consciousness and Eternal Life

Consciousness is the part of the human psyche that is spiritual and indestructible. It is the part of our human makeup that houses the *one life* of God—the life that never dies but only changes forms. Therefore every human being is, at his or her core, eternal and immortal.

The problem is that we fail to identify with that core essence of our being and choose instead, through ignorance and the darkness of the Adam mind, to identify ourselves with other temporal aspects of our psyche, such as our ego, intellect, emotions, and physical body. These aspects of humanhood are not eternal, but rather are subject to the dictates of time and space. Thus by identifying with them, we open the door to such plagues as death, disease, and old age. The truth about human beings is that when we die our consciousness or soul lives on, but having identified ourselves with all the temporal aspects of our psyche since birth we cannot see this and instead come to fear the death of the body as the ultimate annihilation of our being.

Identification then becomes a crucial element of truth, which in turn either promotes consciousness evolution or hinders it. The more our identity is bound up with the temporal aspects of our psyche, the greater our fear of death will be. This overweening fear of death will then extend to other areas of our persona, so that we find ourselves afraid of anything that might cause or hasten death—that is, just about any and everything. This has been the collective consciousness of our species since time immemorial. In the Bible the warning about temporal identification was given to Adam in no uncertain terms: "You will surely die." (Genesis 2:17). Wrong identification was also linked to the knowledge of good and evil or viewing life in terms of dualities. Together these have comprised the collective consciousness of man—a consciousness that has been aptly named *Adamic*—for the past six thousand years. And this Adamic consciousness has been responsible for our fear-driven way of life. It has done this through the wrongful identification with temporal aspects of our human psyche and the misdirected over valuation of the mental faculty of judging between dualities.

Meanwhile our created mandate has not changed one iota. We were created with an eternal soul housed within our psyche. This is the truth of our being. But our conscious awareness has been led astray, pulled down into the mire of the Adam mind. Thus to say that we have been out of touch with the reality of *what is* is not overstating the matter. Certainly we have been caught up in all manner of misperception and mis-valuation, and these deviations from the truth have taken their toll on the quality of human life.

The deep seat of our human consciousness is eternal and of divine essence. That is what Jesus meant when he said that the kingdom of God is within you. (Luke 17:21). Therefore whenever human consciousness is expressive of truth, the dominant characteristic of that expression will be oneness or God-union. On the other hand, if human consciousness is filled with lies, distortions, and wrong beliefs, that which we express outwardly will logically be something less than eternal oneness. In fact, depending on the nature of the wrong belief we have embraced, it could be a lot less.

The seat of human consciousness has not changed, but the character of human consciousness has become expressive of lies and distortions. Ideally, the seat of consciousness and the character of consciousness ought to be in harmonious alignment. Such an alignment in our psyche would be the fulfillment of what Jesus called *knowing the truth*. We would not only realize the truth about our eternal nature; we would also express that realization in the character of our consciousness, which would in turn lead to the ultimate liberation and fulfillment of the human condition. It would be a condition free from sin, disease, lack, and death.

But the character of human consciousness has been sabotaged by the Adam mind. Instead of harmonious alignment and wholeness in our psyche, we must accept lives that are fractured and dysfunctional. Through the inheriting of the Adam mind, we have denied our eternal essence and learned to identify with a false mental construct called ego. We have valued the independent mental faculty of judging between dualities above all other human functions. This willful valuation of the illusion of independence has turned us into a race of prodigals. Instead of union with God, the character of our consciousness expresses ultimate separation. Little have we understood that this stance of prodigal separation has so alienated us from our true nature that it has been tantamount to a declaration of war within the individual human psyche.

The present Adamic character of human consciousness is in direct opposition to our created mandate. Instead of experiencing eternal life, we find ourselves obsessed with death. Instead of oneness with God and all created life forms, we cling to the emptiness of independent prodigality. Instead of inner peace and harmony, we have become fractured and alienated from our own created makeup. Is it any wonder that the conditions of our world reflect this inharmonious state?

We are all familiar with the character of Adamic consciousness, because it has been the dominant character of human society for the past six thousand years. Thus we have grown calloused to its detrimental impact. We have grown to accept disease, old age, and death as inevitabilities. We have become desensitized to the suffering and misery all around us. We have learned to live with war and violence. And we have taken to heart the idea that separation from God in the form of independent prodigality is a more highly evolved state than God-union. This is the mindset of modern man. When will we wake up and realize that it is a mindset reflective of insanity?

What then can we do to effectuate change? We can consciously reject Adamic consciousness and thereby root it out of the human psyche. We can release the restraints that have been holding back our collective evolutionary unfoldment. This will involve saying *no* to the age-old status quo initiative of profit-over-life. And finally we can embrace the testimony of truth as being absolute and inviolable. These things are not too difficult for us. In fact, they would require little strength or effort. Enlightenment is not burdensome, for the nature of light is that it shines in naturally when the closed windows and doors that have been blocking it are opened.

Chapter Two

The Parable as a Truth Teaching

Truth is absolute, whether it pertains to the makeup of the human psyche or some other phenomenon in the natural created universe. The teaching of truth is an unparalleled power for change, because it is a power unto consciousness development, which in turn holds the key to external manifestation.

The prevailing secular view of truth is that it is a relative concept. But even among those who accept truth as absolute many stumble, because they mistakenly imagine that truth must by definition be highly complex and voluminous. The reason for this false idea has its roots in an over valuation of human intellectual capacity. On account of our fascination with intellectual process, we consider that a weighty conjecture must have greater worth and legitimacy than a light one. But when it comes to truth, this maxim is faulty. Truth is simple and pure. Therefore the teaching of truth is a simple and pure matter. It can best be accomplished through the telling of simple life vignettes or parables. This then has been the most oft used device for those wishing to inculcate spiritual truth.

Many people view Jesus' extensive use of the parabolic method of teaching as a justification for believing that what he was imparting was too basic and childish to appeal to a modern sophisticated intellect. But nothing could be further from the truth. Jesus' finely crafted use of the parable as a teaching device revealed that he was a full-blown enlightened master. The proof of this is the fact that for two thousand years men have been discussing and dissecting Jesus' parables looking for hidden meanings, with the interpretation arrived at by one rarely being shared by another. Rather Jesus' parables speak a specific word of truth to each individual, based on that individual's state of consciousness and readiness to receive. This quality of individually tailored impartation makes the parable the perfect teaching device for the development of consciousness.

The Bible is filled with parables. Though we most often associate this teaching method with Jesus and the New Testament, the fact is that it was widely used by enlightened Hebrew prophets and mystics long before Jesus' day. Thus the Old Testament is not only rife with parables; its entire tone and emphasis is parabolic. What does this mean? That the events and people described in the pages of the Old Testament actually have this hidden agenda. The Old Testament narratives, which we tend to read in a strictly historical context, were in fact written as truth teachings. This makes them parabolic in tone. In the New Testament we encounter parables in the form of fables or made-up stories involving made-up people and events. In the Old Testament we read of real people and real historical events, the recounting of which comprise *living parables*.

Fundamentalist Christians and Orthodox Jews alike often miss the significance of the Old Testament's parabolic tone. They read it as a history book, rich in law, imagery, and intrigue but short on spiritual teaching. The characters were historically authentic, and their lives were lived in the same spirit of personal destiny and individual aspiration as our own lives are. In other words, they were not aware that their lives comprised a living parable anymore than you or I would be. They had the same passions, struggles, and philosophical dilemmas that you and I have. And yet, their lives and experiences did become the stuff of spiritual truth teaching, and that means that they were highly efficacious for consciousness development.

The Parable of the Garden

The story at the beginning of the Book of Genesis about the exploits of a man named Adam and his wife Eve in the Garden of Eden is not only parabolic in tone; it is a foundational spiritual teaching that sheds light on this entire age of human initiative. Whether or not Adam and Eve were real people is of no real consequence. Rather it is as a parabolic teaching that this story stands, with its goal being the evolution of human consciousness.

The mystics who were responsible for passing this story down through verbal generational transmission (ultimately to be written down by Moses) were intent on opening men's spiritual faculties, not as has often been thought, on teaching us about the origin of our species and the advent of original sin. When this is understood, it matters little whether Adam was the first man to walk on this planet or that his moral choices were less than upright. What is significant is that Adam and Eve were portrayed as human archetypes who experienced forays into the realm of consciousness that are plainly typical of our species.

In the parable we read of two very distinct states of consciousness. These are described to us through symbolism and the characters' choices and actions. With a poignantly prophetic emphasis these two states of consciousness are presented to the human archetypes for them to either embrace or reject. What makes this prophetic is that these same two states of consciousness have been presented as potential realities to every man and woman that has ever lived throughout this age. They have in fact been the only two reality views available to us. Moreover, each of these states of consciousness comes with a list of repercussions or demonstrations associated with following that particular path. Thus we who are alive six thousand years later can now look back and verify the veracity of each prophecy and warning brought to Adam's consciousness in the garden.

The two states of consciousness presented to Adam and Eve were the state we now call *Adamic* (with its emphasis on the knowledge of good and evil and prodigality) and the state of oneness or God union, in which God is recognized as all and in all (that which I have called *the new consciousness* in this book). Since consciousness development is always progressive and irreversible, there is no real significance to the narrative's presentation of the enlightened consciousness first. Attributing significance to this aspect of the narrative's presentation has given rise to the moral imperative that Adam and Eve *fell* from grace. But since consciousness evolution is irreversible this could not be true. If they had once embraced the enlightened consciousness of God union, it would have been impossible for them to fall away. Rather what is more likely is that Adam and Eve were presented with these two states of consciousness as *choices*. Then as the story describes, they subsequently rejected the enlightened consciousness in favor of Adamic consciousness. There were no moral implications to their choice. Rather it was strictly based on natural attraction and what felt like the best fit for them at the time and in their present state of spiritual evolution. Therefore there are in actuality only two essential truths being taught in this parable. One is that the human archetypes were presented with a choice between these two states of consciousness. And the second is that they chose the state of mental judgment (the knowledge of good and evil) and independent prodigality (that is, separation from God). Only as a secondary teaching does this parable go on to describe the binding repercussions involved in their choice—a description that has proven to be remarkably accurate.

None of these factors existed as condemnatory moral imperatives. But Adam and Eve's choice carried with it moral implications that would be recognized later. For example, the fact that their choice was made based on attraction and emotion instead of reason could certainly be looked at in hindsight as a kind of beguilement. Also the lure of prodigality might well be viewed as a temptation. And of course sin came into play, because duality and prodigality are unnatural and unlawful mindsets. But at the time that they made their choice, they were not conscious of any of this. Therefore they were on moral high ground.

Once the consciousness of God union was rejected by the human archetypes, God became invisible and imperceptible to human sensory function. Then as the prodigal mindset took root in the collective psyche, the idea of experiencing unbroken fellowship with God became increasingly unrealistic and fantastic. In its place the human concept of God became anthropomorphic and hopelessly distorted. The truth about God could no longer be ascertained, because the Adam mind infused the black and white truth with the blinding colors of hurt, fear, and mistrust.

The root cause of all the negative repercussions that were to befall humans on account of Adam and Eve's choice is the sense of separation from God. Had they embraced the consciousness of God union, the human race would have never known sin, disease, poverty, or death. But even after being warned, they decided to reject God union. There were a couple of possible reasons for this. It might have been that they undervalued the idea of being able to have unbroken fellowship with God, or the lure of prodigality might have been too strong for them. But in all likelihood their choice was made simply based on the fact that the consciousness of duality and prodigality struck them as being a better fit for them at that stage of their spiritual development, while the consciousness of God union appeared to them to be too lofty.

And so their choice was made. Immediately, they felt shame and sought to cover their nakedness. Then when faced with the prospect of having to endure God's presence, they hid themselves among the trees of the garden.

It did not take long for Adam and Eve's choice of consciousness to become well defined. The mental function of judging between good and evil dominated their perception. Everything now appeared to them contrasted by its opposite—good and evil, light and darkness, love and hate, etc. This dualistic tendency led to the belief in the balance of power. Evil was not only one side of the good-evil coin; it was a power that rivaled good and needed to constantly be opposed and kept in check. This gave rise to a war-like social climate in the human community. In its obsession to overcome evil, good often resorted to the role of crusader. Evil responded by exposing good's attempts at crusade as being just as bellicose as anything evil might do. The fear of being overcome by evil power led to many pagan forms of worship and superstitious beliefs. Suddenly man decided he needed God after all. There was just one problem. The truth about God had by this time become so distorted that the real God could not be found by men. And without God on their side, the war against evil became a strictly human undertaking.

Prodigality is a godless state. To try to include God in the prodigal picture is religious hypocrisy. When Adam and Eve realized this, they had no choice but to forget about God and accept the fact that their universe would from that time forward be a strictly human one. This is represented in the parable by their expulsion from the garden. The garden represented the fruitful demonstration of the consciousness of God union. The conditions for fruitfulness there were perfect, and the fruit was abundant and good. But outside the garden just the opposite was true. The conditions were severe and blighted. The ground was like flint. Breaking up this fallow ground in order to survive could only be accomplished by the sweat of Adam's brow. This unnatural physical strain then opened the door to disease and death, while man's knowledge of and adherence to God's law became more and more compromised by his desperate plight.

Other Old Testament Parables

After Adam and Eve were banished from the garden, they had two sons: Cain and Abel. These two offspring turned out to be like opposites of one another. This development was expressive of Adamic consciousness' dualistic quality. But it also revealed that man's collective destiny was not yet written in stone.

Cain's uncompromising, unwavering, and almost militant adoption of his father's consciousness represented a budding status quo force, while Abel's instinctual embracing of the consciousness of God union became a viable alternative and gave human beings an extension concerning this important decision. Through Abel, mankind was once again given the chance to make the new consciousness its collective mandate. And Abel had more going for him in this regard than Adam had had in the garden. Whereas Adam had displayed a kind of natural antipathy to God consciousness, Abel seemed to have just the opposite experience. Showing no resistance whatsoever, he embraced the new consciousness wholeheartedly and with alacrity. In other words, for Abel the new consciousness was a perfect fit.

Thus there arose the very real hope that mankind as a collective unit could now distance itself from Adam's choice and adopt the new consciousness after all. There was only one problem. Cain had already gained the vision that his father's dualistic prodigal consciousness was to become the collective consciousness of the human race. His passionate defense of all that Adamic consciousness represented and promised made little sense to Abel. This was because Cain did not tell Abel all that was in his heart. The reason he had become so attached to his father's way was that he was strong, and strength was the key to success in the Darwinian climate of prodigality. Therefore Cain had already succumbed to the temptation of Darwinism. His fate was already decided, and the last thing he wanted was a world of God united souls exposing his wicked intent.

At first the fact that Abel was his brother by blood kept Cain from doing anything rash. But then at some point he felt so threatened by the prospect of Abel's consciousness spreading and becoming the collective mandate that he began to plot Abel's ruin. He vowed to himself to deal with the *Abel problem* forcefully and with the utmost finality and looked for an opportunity to do so. Eventually this opportunity was forthcoming, and Cain took Abel's life.

With Abel physically removed from the scene, all that remained of his consciousness was the testimony of another aborted chance for human beings to choose God consciousness as their collective mandate. Adamic consciousness was once again in the driver's seat. Cain's status quo movement quickly became firmly entrenched in human society. And as an added bonus, men now saw the expediency in implementing new methodologies for securing and maintaining their control. With Cain as their role model, other status quo defenders learned to deal swiftly and shrewdly with any outcropping of the new consciousness that appeared in their midst. With cruel strength, deceptive practices, and even legislation banning the *Abel mindset*, they hoped to rid the earth of it once and for all. But despite all their efforts, they were unable to completely blot out Abel's legacy. Therefore the testimony of the new consciousness lived on.

Somehow Noah heard of this testimony and was initiated into the consciousness of God union, even though he lived in a time when the cruelty of the status quo was perhaps at its greatest cohesion. Alone and often persecuted, Noah learned to commune with God inwardly and keep silent about his unique inner life when around others. In this way he was warned about the coming flood. Living in a region that was nowhere near the sea, Noah set about the daunting task of building a great ark. One can only imagine the ridicule he endured from the members of his community for this act. "Noah is mad," they must have thought. But Noah continued to build the ark unto completion. And it was a good thing too. For, no sooner had he finished it than the rains came, and the water soon covered the whole earth.

The primary teaching of this *living parable* is that Adamic consciousness was shown to be extremely tenacious, based on the fact that even though the population of the world was virtually wiped out, in almost no time after the flood waters subsided things were back to normal. Had Noah and his wife been the only humans to be saved in the ark, it might have been different. The new consciousness might have found that its time had come. But in the parable we read that Noah's family entered the ark with him. This consisted of his three sons and their wives, and it was through these that the post-diluvian human scene once again came under the sway of Adamic consciousness. Like déjà vu, a status quo movement was once again established and soon began to thrive. Interestingly, this parable also uses the symbol of nakedness to show that the knowledge of good and evil, though not as dominant in Noah, had clearly become the prevailing mindset of his sons. It tells how Noah once became drunk after drinking the wine from a vineyard he had planted and proceeded to lay down in his tent *uncovered*. When his sons discovered their father's nakedness, they carefully covered him, turning their faces the other way in their shame. Thus the story of Adam and Eve's nakedness in the garden was reenacted, replete with the belief that nakedness was evil and covering it was good.

Many centuries later another lone human being stumbled upon the new consciousness. This took place in a world that had begun to accept the status quo's views to such an extent that these were considered truth or reality. In other words, the society of men had come under the control of a *subjective reality system*. It was during this epoch that truth became lost and was replaced with *concepts of expediency*. This propaganda fueled societal climate had been the brainchild of some especially zealous status quo defenders, operating as a political hierarchy. Thus its purpose and goal were entirely geared to the perpetuation of the status quo. Cain's violent solution to dealing with Abel's threat to the status quo had been one method for control, but the implementation of a subjective reality system was even more effective. Its subtle, non-coercive guise showed a far greater sophistication and long-range vision. It showed that the status quo was never going to relinquish its control willingly but rather would so twist the reality of human life that anyone who dared to think their own thoughts would be branded a madman.

The parable of the Tower of Babel plainly delineates this development in human society. It describes the state of the world as having one language and culture, which is to say that it had one prevailing reality view. Furthermore the dominant mindset among the people was clearly an arrogant brand of prodigality or the willful and proud separation from God. "Come let us build ourselves a city, with a tower that reaches to the heavens and make a name for ourselves," the people voiced as one (Genesis 11:4). They already had made a name for themselves among all people, but now they were intent on proving their worth to God and countering God's reality with their own. This is status quo sentiment at the height of arrogance. It is an entire society of men with the mind of Cain, only instead of eradicating any *Abels* in their midst, which they had already succeeded in doing, they now turned their gaze to heaven and challenged the very source of the new consciousness—God!

Though the parable of the tower ends with the humbling of these arrogant men, there is little question that they soon regrouped and continued their control of human society through the ever-expanding influence of the subjective reality system. This was clearly the prevailing climate of human society, when God consciousness came to a man named Abram. The testimony of the new consciousness was so strong in him and the opposition from a status quo society united by a common subjective reality system so intense that the parable of Abraham (as his name later became) begins with him fleeing from the civilized world and making his way to a foreign land that was largely unsettled and uninhabited.

In the land of Canaan by the Mediterranean Sea Abraham was able to develop his consciousness of God union without opposition or persecution. This process of consciousness development is described symbolically in the parable as the act of well digging. Therefore though Abraham had plenty of adventures in his new country, the real emphasis in the narrative is on his spiritual growth. His deep level of commitment, freedom of expression, and the extensive length of his lifespan made him the most highly developed proponent of the new consciousness to live upon the earth up to this point.

Thus the essential teaching of this parable is that God consciousness develops incrementally and is highly responsive to one's degree of commitment and dedication. Abraham's life experience showed that any man that was dedicated and persistent could excel in the demonstration of the new consciousness. He could live a life of realized oneness with God to such an extent that God's power would flow through him for the healing and enlightenment of others—a demonstration later perfected by

Jesus of Nazareth. This demonstration of God union has always been consistent in its outworking. It is the fullness of human life, reflected by the fruits of the Spirit—joy, love, perfect health, abundant supply, and redemptive soul cleansing.

The Old Testament does not credit Abraham with the working of miraculous signs and wonders, but that does not mean his demonstration was void of power. Abel never did miracles either, but the testimony of his developed consciousness was so strong that it drove his brother mad with jealousy. Like Abel, Abraham's demonstration was to leave such a powerful testimony about the truth of the new consciousness that it would not only be reintroduced into human society; it would spread throughout and eventually leaven the whole lump. Thus the teaching of this parable is also that it only takes one man moving in the truth of the new consciousness to impact the whole world and ultimately usher in the new age. In this sense Abraham became the forerunner for the concept of messianic salvation that was later to come.

Of course, it helped tremendously that Abraham had left the civilized society of men in Ur of Chaldea and settled in the land of Canaan, where there was no existing status quo movement to oppose him or the overpowering influence of world mesmerism to defile him. Thus we learn yet another lesson from this parable: sometimes in order for a truly great spiritual work to be born in our hearts we must take the path of least resistance, shun the mainstream, and seek to dwell in solitude and obscurity.

And so through Abraham the new consciousness reappeared upon the earth, and before long it began to spread. In the incubator of the land of Canaan Abraham's son and grandson took up his mantle and dug their own wells of spiritual truth. After that Jacob's twelve sons were all initiated into the new consciousness and began to live spiritually focused lives. But then something unforeseen happened. A famine fell upon the land of Canaan that was so severe, it forced Jacob's entire clan to relocate to the nearby wealthy nation of Egypt.

The Parable of Israel

Egypt was not like the land of Canaan. In fact, in terms of cultural modernity and sophistication it was more closely aligned to Babylon—the land that Abraham had once fled from. It was a thriving world center with a strong subjective reality system as its dominant myth and a powerful status quo political hierarchy. Thus while the fledgling community of new consciousness proponents found the solution to their physical survival there, for the first time they were exposed to the proactive opposition of human reality myths and a status quo initiative. In other words, the dynamic of Cain and Abel was reenacted yet again with the spirit of Cain taking the form of a nation called Egypt and the spirit of Abel being embodied by the sons of Israel (as Jacob's name had been changed to).

As with Cain and Abel, some time passed during which the Israelites and Egyptians coexisted with a degree of tolerance. But eventually the status quo hierarchy in that land predictably became threatened and hostile. When this occurred, it resulted in cruel enslavement for Israel, with their ultimate fate being slated for annihilation.

In the meantime Israel had become a small nation in its own right. Their community had increased in number to nearly one million. And amazingly, though now so vast in population, they had managed to retain at least certain elements of the new consciousness teaching handed down to them by their forefathers, not to mention that they were also united through oppression and suffering. This was clearly an unprecedented phenomenon in the history of mankind. Never had the testimony of those individual trailblazers Abel, Noah, Abraham, Isaac, and Jacob been embraced by an entire community of souls. Now the Egyptian status quo hierarchy was kicking itself. What had they done? Through tolerance and slackness, this nation of Cainites had allowed the testimony of Abel to thrive right under its nose. Finally a pharaoh took power who vowed not only to put a stop to this trend but also to cruelly reverse it. Cain was once again poised and looking for an opportunity to murder his brother.

But this nation of Abelites had learned a thing or two about these dynamics. They had developed a rich national heritage that was tied to the land that had been so beneficent to their forefathers and conducive to the development of their spiritual consciousness—a land that their forefathers had called home for two centuries. Thus the more bitter their enslavement in Egypt became, the more the Israelites found themselves clinging to the hope of one day returning to the land of Canaan and once again putting down roots there. Just as Abraham had once taken the initiative to leave the civilized world of men in order to find freedom of worship and consciousness development, so the Israelites had now become reconciled to the same fate. If only they could! Unfortunately, the Egyptians were now so thoroughly bent on their destruction, that they refused to let the Israelites leave.

In the end what saved the people was the very consciousness that set them apart and had caused the Egyptians to persecute them. The demonstration of power came through a man, but it was in truth the demonstration of spiritual consciousness. It was therefore the power of God.

The man through whom this demonstration came was one of their own named Moses. He was a no-nonsense character who took on the role of Israel's deliverer as a matter of personal destiny. In fact, after living the first forty years of his life as a prince in Pharaoh's house, he became suddenly so dedicated to the cause of Israel's liberation that he was willing to devote the remainder of his life to it.

Instinctually, Moses fled from Egypt and took up residence in a wilderness region located halfway between Egypt and Canaan. The purpose for this self-banishment was that he might dig his own spiritual well and learn from God the intricacies of the new consciousness in the solitary environs of the wilderness. In this way he hoped to become strong enough to be able to return to Egypt and force Pharaoh's hand—not through human strength but rather by the Spirit of God. Thus the wilderness became a sort of training ground for him. For another full forty years he listened to the silence and learned to trust God's inner presence and guidance. Then in the fullness of time he did indeed feel empowered to return to Egypt and deliver the Israelites from their cruel bondage.

Moses' demonstration of the new consciousness, replete with many miraculous signs and wonders, was the most highly developed of any man that had walked the earth up to that time. But this did not mean that he was somehow set apart from other human beings. It only meant that he had worked harder and gone further in the development of spiritual consciousness. Though the circumstances surrounding his demonstration were unique, it nonetheless would prove to be consistent with the demonstrations of all other enlightened masters. The spiritual power of God that came through Moses was the same power that Jesus would later invoke. It was the power to heal the sick, raise the dead, deliver the captives, relieve the oppressed, and lift up the downtrodden.

Apostasy

After the descendants of Israel had resettled in the land of Canaan, they were indeed free to follow their hearts and unfold their national and religious destinies. They were no longer subject to the status quo's cruelty. Just as their forefather Abraham had once done, they found Canaan to be a haven from the onslaught of world mesmerism. There they could prosper and thrive, and at first their fortunes definitely seemed on the upswing. But then slowly but surely problems began to arise. Strangely, these problems no longer had their source in outside oppression; rather they came from within their own ranks.

What they were discovering was that the higher consciousness was not actually transferable genetically. Religious rituals and national aspirations could be passed on to the next generation, but spiritual consciousness had to be taken to heart by each and every individual in order for it to continuously infuse the collective entity with vibrant life and blessing. Though they had been the world's first nation to be founded and built upon spiritual principles—the testimonies of Abraham, Isaac, and Jacob in regards to the new consciousness—working out their national destiny in their new homeland in harmony with those principles required that each Israelite dig his or her own spiritual well. And eventually this requirement became a snare and a curse to them. Each new generation rebelled a little more against the burden of having to be spiritually oriented.

The apostasy of Israel ultimately became epidemic. When this occurred, Adamic consciousness once again took control of the collective destiny. True, it took on a new look, as if to disguise itself. It donned sacerdotal robes and claimed devotion to a vast array of religious and legal regulations. It tried to pass itself off as the true faith of Abraham. But all one had to do was to look closely to see that Israel's value system had gone the way of the world. Human intelligence and strength were the attributes that propelled an individual to a position of prominence, wealth, and influence. And as this societal restructuring took place, a new status quo movement became entrenched. With their mouths these new religionists professed to be Abraham's descendants, but by their deeds it was evident that their hearts belonged to the father of all status quo sentiment, Cain.

As the centuries passed, things began to look bleak again for the new consciousness. The status quo movement in Israel had become just as ruthless and deadly as its heathen manifestations.

Prophets were raised up who testified against the godless sham of a religion that had replaced the new consciousness. But one by one these were removed from the scene, usually via the act of religiously justifiable homicide. Thus the testimony of the new consciousness became more and more muted.

But then we read in the Old Testament of the ministry of a great prophet named Elijah. Powerful in the consciousness of God-presence, Elijah was hated and persecuted by the people of his day. At one point he was hunted down like the worst sort of criminal. Despairing over the apostate condition of the nation, Elijah cried out to God, saying, "The Israelites have rejected your covenant, broken down your altars, and put your prophets to death with the sword. I am the only one left, and now they are trying to kill me too." (1 Kings 19:10). Then this answer came to him, "Yet I reserve seven thousand in Israel—all whose knees have not bowed down to Baal and whose mouths have not kissed him." (1 Kings 19:18). This word was like music to Elijah's ears, not that his own life might be spared but rather that God was not going to let the testimony of the new consciousness be entirely extinguished. True, it was being forced underground—again. But it had not and would not be destroyed. It had out of necessity become a remnant phenomenon.

Chapter Three

The Testimony of Jesus

Seven centuries passed with the new consciousness surviving as an underground remnant phenomenon. The testimony of Abel was restricted to Abraham's descendants, for they were the only ones who had preserved a teaching about the one true God. They may not have taken this teaching completely to heart, but they nonetheless preserved it. This is because their religion venerated men who had once dug deep wells of spiritual salvation—Abraham, Isaac, Jacob, and Moses. Thus inadvertently they had allowed the remnant theology to survive.

Then something wonderful beyond description happened in our world. Just when the status quo movement linked to Cain had conquered nearly every corner and crevice of the known world, a savior of the remnant line of Abel was born—Jesus of Nazareth. Growing up right under the noses of a ruthless status quo hierarchy, Jesus reached the age of mature manhood. Then for three years he conducted a well-documented public teaching and healing ministry. Eventually the status quo defenders got to him and hung him on a Roman cross. But the damage to their cause had already been done. The teaching of Jesus not only entered the world; it went forth with guarded precision. Then like an unquenchable wildfire, it broke out beyond the borders of the land of Canaan and changed our world beyond recognition. In fact, it is still burning out of control to this very day. Never had the embodiment of the new consciousness been so concentrated in one man. Never had its demonstration been so irrefutable. Never had its testimony been so indomitable. Through this one man the entire balance of power in the human scene was upended. Once long ago Cain had gained control and established his status quo movement through a murderous agenda. Now it was as if the brother he had once silenced had risen from the dead, never to be subject to silencing again.

Over the course of the past two millennia Jesus of Nazareth has become most prominently associated with the great world religion Christianity. But as prolific as this religious testimony has been, there has actually been a greater testimony in the realm of spiritual consciousness. This testimony of consciousness transcends the religious testimony, because it encompasses both the religious and secular communities. In other words, it is universally human.

The testimony of spiritual consciousness has also been more honest and truthful. What Jesus accomplished during his short ministry has often been distorted and misinterpreted by those bent on religious inculcation. With impure motives, religious zealots have resorted to using the fear of damnation as a weapon of dissemination. But when one views the testimony of Jesus in terms of consciousness, there is no emphasis on coercive dissemination and therefore no recourse to dishonesty.

Another falsehood spread by the religious community has involved the person of Jesus. In our boxed-in Adamic consciousness the predominant explanation for how Jesus performed so many miraculous signs and wonders has been to put forth a doctrine of his divinity. Thus the Church teaches that Jesus was not like other men; he was a sort of God-man. At some point this doctrine inspired not only love and gratitude but worship as well. But here again when we understand that Jesus was not a religious icon but rather a man with a highly developed spiritual consciousness, a sane assessment is achieved. Through this perspective we see that Jesus' works were but the demonstration of his state of consciousness and that because both consciousness and demonstration are scientifically predictable these same works could have been done by any human being moving in that same state of highly developed spiritual consciousness. We also come to understand that no demonstration of higher consciousness has as its primary impetus a sovereign personal divine initiative. Rather God is always the same, and the agenda of spiritual enlightenment needs no sovereign dictate in order to be perpetuated.

What this means is that the Bible, replete with testimonies of faithfulness and remnant persecution, is not so much about God as it is about men. God has always been the same, and God's nature and qualities might well be described in just a few pages. But the true drama found in the Bible involves the thematic stories and accounts of various men and women experiencing the well-trod transformation from Adamic consciousness to the new consciousness of God realization.

When seen in this light, we actually come to value the Bible even more. For when we previously believed that it was mainly a book about divine beings, this belief created a certain distance between the writings and us. But when we realize that the Bible is all about regular people just like you and me, we do not feel so left out of the loop. True, many of the Bible's protagonists experienced wonderful breakthroughs in the realm of consciousness development, but those breakthroughs were never exclusive or superhuman; rather they were scientific and universal. Therefore they were common to man.

Amazingly, this same inspirational quality can be applied to all human historical writings. How simplified human history becomes, when we view it in terms of consciousness development. The real movers and shakers of our species have all been on the same journey—the journey of consciousness development. They have evolved beyond the darkness, smallness, and desperation of the Adam mind and found strength and power emanating from the light of the new consciousness.

The Demonstration of Jesus

Many of the Bible protagonists who experienced the transformation in consciousness from Adamic to God-union demonstrated this transformation through their actions and works. But none of these demonstrations compare to Jesus'. It might then be deduced that though human in every way, Jesus' consciousness development so far surpassed that of other men that he was truly set apart.

There are many different stages of development on the journey of consciousness evolution, and each stage of unfoldment has its own peculiar demonstration. There is, however, a consistency to the nature of all higher consciousness demonstration. The Bible calls this higher consciousness demonstration *doing the works of God*. These works include healing diseases, restoring sight to the blind, making the deaf hear and the lame to walk, etc. But there are even higher degrees of demonstration than these, including raising the dead back to life, reading thoughts as if they had been spoken out loud, seeing into the future, and absolute fearlessness. These higher degrees of demonstration are very rare. They involve not only knowing the truth of God, but knowing it so integrally that one can see through every false appearance and be completely unmoved by every mesmeric human belief.

There have been many demonstrations of a healing consciousness, but never has there been any record of fearlessness and clear seeing to match the demonstration of Jesus. This was his greatest testimony. The truth was so strong in him that no lie or false appearance could endure in his presence. Thus it was not just that Jesus healed people. It was how he healed them that set him apart. When Jesus healed he did not use some formula or verbal incantation; neither did he become excited or emotional. Rather he calmly took refuge in the truth of God that was so real to his consciousness.

In Jesus' consciousness God was all and in all, and God was the perfection of being. God was the substance of all form, the cause of all effect, and the source of every manifestation. Therefore any manifestation that did not reflect this God-being was a false appearance. Now it is one thing to have learned this truth, but it is another thing to know it so thoroughly that one *never* doubts it and *never* feels fear.

When we are dealing with a God that is invisible and appearances that seem so real, it takes a very high consciousness to not waver in regards to spiritual truth. Moreover, after thousands of years in which Adamic consciousness has injected human life with the fear of death, it takes a very high consciousness to be immune to fear. These attributes are what set apart Jesus' demonstration and made it unique. Jesus never doubted what he knew to be true, and his absolute mastery over the fear of death was revealed when he willingly submitted to the cross.

In the religious world Jesus' demonstration is attributed to his divinity, not to developed spiritual consciousness. But the truth is that Jesus' demonstration, while in harmony with the divine will, was actually more human than divine. He did not receive power from on high at the moment he needed it. He did not entreat God to act on his behalf. The power was already residing in him through his own state of developed spiritual consciousness. Therefore his demonstration had little to do with God, except for the fact that a highly developed spiritual consciousness will always do the will of God and cannot do otherwise.

Jesus was well aware of these dynamics. Never did he claim to be divine. He knew exactly who he was—a human being with a very highly developed spiritual consciousness. Therefore his teaching was compassionate and practical. It never created a distance between himself and other people. Jesus never took the condescending attitude that a personal God to whom he had special access was working through him to bless the people. Rather he taught: greater works than these shall *you* do. Such a teaching only bears fruit when seen in the light of consciousness development.

We are human beings. None of us can become God. But we can aspire to having the same mind that Jesus had—that is, the same level of conscious union with God. And not only can we aspire to this goal; we can realize it. That is what the new consciousness is all about. It is the attaining of the same mind that was in Christ Jesus. And though this attaining may not come easily for us, it is entirely within our potential. Then based on scientific principles, once our consciousness has expanded to where we share the mind of Jesus, we will surely share his demonstration as well.

The Vision of Jesus

Jesus was a visionary and a revolutionary. His three-year ministry was certainly wonderful beyond description, but he actually had his vision set on a more expansive purpose. Healing diseases and being an instrument for the redemptive principle of God to work through were glorious demonstrations, but they were not the full extent of Jesus' work. His vision was so lofty and far reaching that no one in his day could even conceive of it. His was the vision that the new consciousness would one day encircle the globe and raise mankind out of its age-long degradation to the Adam mind.

When Jesus looked out on the distressed multitudes that followed him from place to place, he did not see them as victims of circumstances, poor health habits, bad luck, the ravages of time, or heredity. He saw them as victims of Adamic consciousness. Though he himself had no trace of Adamic consciousness at work in him, he knew very well what it was and what its resultant outworking tended to be. He knew that the Parable of the Garden spelled it out for all to understand. Adam had accepted a well-defined consciousness of duality (the knowledge of good and evil) and the belief in two powers (a power of evil to rival God). Then he had begun to perceive himself as being separate and cut off from God. At first, it is likely that Adam felt comfortable with this state of consciousness, but eventually even he had to admit that it had become a Pandora's box, through which a great many troubles—described in scripture as the *plagues of Egypt*—came into the world. Furthermore, Jesus had a thorough understanding of the political dynamics that followed Adam's choice. He perceived that when Cain murdered his brother Abel, it set in motion the mass dissemination of Adamic consciousness through force and violence and gave birth to a status quo initiative bent on preserving the societal climate of Darwinian prodigality at all costs—a climatic pattern that has dominated this age of man.

Jesus knew therefore that human society had gotten hopelessly stuck in the pattern established by Cain, so that even when an occasional individual broke through to a higher state he or she was unable to effect change in society at large. Invariably, the status quo movement dealt treacherously with such individuals and squelched or distorted their testimonies, thereby keeping the collective entity in bondage.

All of this had resulted in a societal climate rife with pain and suffering. Human beings had been suffering for so long that they had come to accept this condition as normal and natural. This had been going on for thousands of years. It had nothing to do with being a curse from God. In fact, Jesus often found himself vehemently combating this misconception. Suffering never came from God. Rather it was the direct result of separation from God. It was the fruit of prodigality. "Know a tree by its fruit," he often taught, because it was so clear to him. Adamic consciousness brings forth a harvest of devastation—disease, sin, poverty, and death. It is like any other law of nature. Its working is scientifically inviolable. It does not matter what other variables come into play. Therefore if Adamic consciousness remained entrenched in human society, people would never be able to live suffering-free lives; they would never know life abundant.

Jesus knew that the human body had no will or intelligence of its own. It was not self-acting. Rather it was acted upon by consciousness. Thus Adamic consciousness was literally a killer. Its divided dualistic mindset created a climate of darkness and weakness in the body—a climate wherein dysfunction and disease bred and thrived. Its idolatrous belief in other powers that rival God gave rise to so much fear that it often incapacitated bodily functions. And its insistent clinging to the orientation of prodigality gave impetus to a Darwinian struggle to survive that forced the body to bear all manner of unnatural stresses and strains. All of this threw the delicate balance of the body's intricate organic systems into total shock and disarray.

And so Jesus deduced that the multitudes of sick and deformed people that followed him were really only suffering from one general malaise—Adamic consciousness. He could heal them through his own enlightened consciousness, but unless they evolved spiritually and left Adamic consciousness behind, their ailments would return. Thus Jesus the visionary knew that the healing work he was doing was not enough. What the people needed most was to be raised up into the new consciousness. When that happened, not only would their lives become suffering-free, but they would also become healers in their own right.

This then was his truest calling. And it was not just for the people of Israel that he carried this burden. Rather his vision was a universal one, which included all mankind. The new consciousness is never exclusive in its manifestation; it never chooses one race or people over another. Neither is suffering endemic. It does not take a keen eye to see that it is a worldwide phenomenon. And Adamic consciousness is also universal right now. Therefore the new consciousness must go out into the entire world in order for human suffering to once and for all be eradicated.

Jesus saw all this very plainly. He saw the devastation of Adamic consciousness all around him. He saw the corrupt agenda of the status quo holding the people in bondage to suffering. Everyone was groping in the dark; life was like a bad dream. How was he to wake them from this dream? He knew that his efforts would be staunchly opposed by the ruling status quo hierarchy. And yet he also could perceive that he had a ministerial window of three years in which to make inroads in the collective consciousness. How then was he to best use these years?

Clearly Jesus was set apart from the multitudes. It was not his intention to be different, but his consciousness was so far above other people that he might as well have been from another planet. He was so full of goodness and light that suffering was not a part of his personal experience in any way, shape, or form. In contrast, the consciousness of the people was so deeply mired in fear and desperation that suffering was a constant reality for them. How was he to bridge this huge gap between them? His compassion knew no bounds, because he saw that the future of Adam's race depended on whether or not he could help the people evolve in consciousness. Therefore the scripture was fulfilled in him: "A bruised reed he would not break." (Isaiah 42:3). Rather he was full of tenderness as he performed his healing work.

His teaching also reflected this compassionate approach. He did not appeal to men's intellects, like the scribes and Pharisees did. For, he did not want to alienate those for whom learning and memorizing came difficultly. The truth he taught was simple and pure. It did not build men up falsely. Rather it sought to raise men's consciousness and in this way to deliver them from their doubts and fears. To this end he often employed the parabolic method of teaching, for this method, more than any other teaching method, is best suited to consciousness development.

Basically, Jesus taught the way of the new consciousness, but out of compassion he used imagery and terminology that the people of his day were familiar and comfortable with. The people of Israel had preserved the knowledge of God as one God, but they had allowed the pagan notions of the heathen nations around them to creep in and infiltrate the purity of their faith. The result of this infiltration was a distorted view of the One. Thus by the time Jesus arrived on the scene they had largely come to view God as personal, capricious, and vengeful—a God hostile to man, short on mercy and heavy on judgment. In short, the Jewish God had morphed into a kind of anthropomorphic tyrant.

Therefore much of the emphasis of Jesus' teaching was a kind of gentle correction of the current misconceptions. He did away with all notions of divine caprice, wrath and judgment and portrayed God as consistently and scientifically benevolent. He brought God down from a high and distant heavenly throne to an active Spirit in the midst of the people. He also did away with all notions of exclusivity and favoritism on God's part, teaching instead that God's rain fell on the just and the unjust alike. He exposed human self-righteousness by refuting the idea that human beings are capable of the kind of goodness that belongs to God alone. He even rebuked someone for referring to him as *good*, saying, "Why do you call me good? No one is good except God alone." (Luke 18:19). Finally he taught tirelessly that God is not responsible for man's suffering. God is not our enemy, but our savior.

Jesus' Greatest Demonstration

There is one teaching that all those who have ever been mired in Adamic consciousness need to hear most. It is the teaching of reconciliation with God.

The very crux of the Adam mentality is an inviolable sense of separation from God. This is the true root cause of all human suffering. And what makes this such a poignant predicament is that this sense of separation is not even real. There is no separation between God and man on God's part and never has been. There is only this *perceived* sense of separation on man's part. There is the unconscious belief that our sins and bad thoughts cause a wedge between God and us. Thus the sense of separation we carry around when under the sway of Adamic consciousness is actually illusory. It is nothing more than a misperception or false superstitious belief.

The dynamic of sin and guilt in the human psyche has become extremely complex. Oftentimes these manifest as subconscious impulses. They impact our choices, our behavior, and our emotional state without our being aware of it. The teaching of reconciliation is the antidote to this poison, but because our condition tends to be buried in the subconscious realms of our minds the teaching sometimes fails to get to the root of the problem. This is especially true if it is presented in word only, without any accompanying imagery or demonstration.

It is for this reason that Jesus came to the realization that ultimately his words and even his miraculous signs would not be enough to set the people free and raise them into the new consciousness—the consciousness of reconciliation and union with God. This realization was confirmed by the way that the people responded to his ministerial efforts. Jesus could tell that they were not really getting it. They were just taking the help that Jesus offered and going on their merry way. And it was this confirmation that cemented in his mind the necessity of dying on the cross.

Jesus saw that his death on the cross would impact the collective human psyche in the realm of consciousness in a way that his words and miracles did not. How? It would create a haunting visual image that would work like leaven in a person's inner world and little by little undermine the resistance of the Adam mind. Then after his death and resurrection the teaching of the apostles would combine the imagery of the cross with the message of reconciliation, and the stranglehold of sin and guilt would be broken. All this was prophetically foreseen by John the Baptist, when he referred to Jesus as the *Lamb of God who takes away the sin of the world* (John 1:29). Jesus also spoke of it in these terms: "If I be lifted up [on the cross] I will draw all men unto me." (John 12:32). And it was through the strengthening that came with this revelation that he set his sights on the cross and did not waver.

What made the imagery of the cross so profound and powerful? Even a hardened criminal who was crucified alongside of him could see that Jesus had done nothing to deserve death. In fact, of all people Jesus deserved death the least on account of his good deeds, if nothing else. Not only this, but death on the cross was no ordinary death. It was the most torturous cruel form of death devised by men in the history of our world. It tortured its victim by stretching his body downward through the law of gravity, until every bone and joint was severed and out-of-place. Only after hours of excruciating pain did the victim finally expire.

Jesus hung on the cross as one who was innocent, meek, and mild. "Which of you can convict me of sin?" he had once asked his antagonists—a question to which no one could give an answer. Thus when applying the message of reconciliation to the imagery of him hanging on the cross, he became the quintessential sacrificial lamb, dying for the forgiveness of sin. And in keeping with the typology foreshadowed by the Jewish ritual of animal sacrifice, he was without blemish or defect. He was the perfect lamb, enduring the shame of the cross in order to reconcile us to God. And the fact that he was willing to be tortured and die *for us* and *in our place* is the image that has haunted mankind for two thousand years. It is truly the love of the savior. When taken in to human consciousness, the hard heart of the prodigal begins to melt, being overcome with grief and sorrow, and we are made receptive to God's Spirit.

The imagery of the cross was all that was needed to undermine Adamic consciousness and weaken its stranglehold upon us, but it is not the power that lifts us into the new consciousness. Rather it is like a necessary first step, in which the Adam mind is once and for all exposed and rejected. The Bible calls this step *repentance*, and nothing further can happen in the arena of consciousness development without it. In Jesus' important parable about the prodigal son we read about this first step in these words: "When he came to his senses. . . ." (Luke 15:17). That is what repentance is in relation to Adamic consciousness; it is a coming to one's senses, nothing more. This step then kick-starts the spiritual journey described in the parable as the *return to the father's house*—a journey in which we cease from our willful prodigality and seek reconciliation with God.

Thus the cross was Jesus' greatest demonstration, accomplishing far more in the realm of consciousness than words or miracles could do. Though it does not, in itself, lead us to the Father's house, it breaks the spell of Adamic consciousness and sets us free to begin the journey. It awakens us from the dream of separation and sets us on the course of full reconciliation with God—the mystical union of the new consciousness.

Chapter Four

The Testimony of the Apostles

After the imagery of the cross has worked in our hearts like leaven and brought us to our senses, we are free to leave our empty prodigal existence behind and move forward to embrace the new consciousness. The question then becomes: what is the way? As the Apostle Thomas voiced after Jesus assured the eleven they instinctively knew the way to the place he was going: "Lord, we don't know where you are going, so how can we know the way?" (John 14:5). In other words, the apostles understood at this point that the gospel of their Lord was all about the development of spiritual consciousness, but like all men who have been mired in Adamic consciousness they simply had no frame of reference for understanding what the new consciousness would be like; neither did they know how to proceed. In answer to Thomas' question, Jesus replied: "I am the way and the truth and the life." (John 14:6). This meant that somehow they were to follow Jesus, but what was to happen once Jesus was taken from them and no longer present with them? Then lest they should despair, Jesus told them: "When he, the Spirit of truth, comes, he will guide you into all truth. . . . Then you will rejoice, and no one will take away your joy." (John 16:13,22). Looking back, we can see that these prophetic words of Jesus did come to pass. The Spirit of truth did come upon the apostles; it did guide them into all truth, and they were subsequently filled with joy as a result. Thus they did end up following Jesus, and after his ascension it was the apostles that took up the mantle of testifying about the new consciousness.

Even after two thousand years most people in the western world are familiar with at least some of Jesus' teaching. And any time we feel so inclined, it is as easy as picking up a copy of the New Testament to add to and expand upon our familiarity. Clearly, when it came to inculcating spiritual truth, Jesus had no rival. But rarely do we consider the labor and commitment that went into insuring that this richness of spiritual truth was preserved and handed down to us. Jesus himself was not responsible for writing down or keeping a record of his teaching. Rather that task fell into the hands of the apostles. Thus it was their diligence and faithfulness that gave us the New Testament. And as it turns out, it is the writing in that book that can act as a kind of road map for us, showing the way to the new consciousness.

It is likely that the apostles did not fully understand the nature or significance of their commission, nor of its timeless durability. The reason for this assessment lies in their adherence to the religious imagery and terminology of their time and place of upbringing. With the exception of the Apostle John, the New Testament writers seemed to have little understanding about spiritual consciousness and the need for consciousness development, at least not in those terms. They did not seem to understand that consciousness development was not a religious pursuit. In their minds consciousness and religion were part of the same non-secular ball of wax. It allowed them to be able to keep separate from the growing mesmerism of Greek and Roman culture that was consuming the entire western world. But to view consciousness development as a universal individual undertaking was beyond their scope, even though this was the teaching of their master. Therefore the power in the testimony of the apostles was really attributable to their faithful handling of Jesus' teaching—a teaching that they themselves did not seem to fully grasp. Even Jesus employed religious imagery and terminology, but this was more in deference to his listeners than due to his own lack of understanding. And it was not dominant. Rather the dominant theme in Jesus' teaching was universal consciousness development, and because the apostles were faithful to let this theme shine through, it became their testimony as well.

The Apostle Paul, however, presents an enigmatic and controversial teaching. As the writer of a large part of the New Testament, Paul jumbles together the Judaic religion he had been trained in with the spiritual message of messianic salvation. Thus what emerges is a kind of religious spirituality, replete with the truth of the new consciousness and a detailed blueprint of how to apply that truth within a religious framework and ecclesiastic structure. Sometimes confusedly, Paul shifts back and forth from a wonderfully inspired expounding of truth to a dry and mundane list of moral exhortations and organizational practicalities.

Unlike the other apostolic writings, Paul's letters do not present the teachings of Jesus in completeness and purity. Rather they venture into interpretive realms, and as a result must be read with discrimination in order to glean the pearls of spiritual truth that testify to the new consciousness.

Apostolic Authority

Their teaching aside, we can deduce that the apostles that had been with Jesus *lived* according to the tenets of the new consciousness. For, we read in the Book of Acts the historical account of a collective experience that took place on the day of Pentecost—that is fifty days after Jesus was crucified. On that morning the apostles were gathered together in one place, when they experienced God's presence as an active indwelling Spirit for the first time. This Spirit came upon them with powerful signs and a definite demonstration. First there came a strange sound like nothing they had ever heard before; then a violent wind swept through the house they were in; and finally, they saw a vision of fiery tongues coming to rest on each of their heads, after which they found themselves able to speak in foreign tongues they had never learned before. (Acts 2:1-4). This experience of receiving God's Spirit as an indwelling presence is the essential initiation of the new consciousness, and it is never a passing phase or fleeting phenomenon. Rather it represents a permanent shift in our spiritual orientation and only displays movement in that it expands toward greater and greater light. Jesus predicted that this experience would soon befall the apostles, and that after it happened they would be permanently changed. He was able to do this based on the scientific law of consciousness development and its subsequent demonstration.

This great event, called *Pentecost* in Christian religious tradition, came about because the apostles were spiritually ready and receptive—a readiness and receptivity that had been cultivated through their time with Jesus. All that it took was for them to be weaned off of their dependency of having Jesus with them in the flesh, which was brought about in the days immediately following his ascension. Jesus foresaw this and instructed them accordingly: "Do not leave Jerusalem, but wait for the gift my Father promised, which you have heard me speak about." (Acts 1:4).

We know that the consciousness of God's presence within them as an indwelling Spirit took root and bore fruit in the lives of the apostles, because not only were they changed after their Pentecostal initiation, but they were greatly empowered ministerially and found themselves performing signs and wonders among the people routinely. This too Jesus had predicted long in advance, when he told them: "Greater works than these will *you* do." (John 14:12). Again, Jesus could foresee this outcome based on scientific probability. The works that the apostles began to do were simply the usual demonstration of the new consciousness. They were the same works Jesus had done.

The great news in all this was that though Jesus was now gone from the human scene, the new consciousness had successfully been passed on to the apostles, like a baton in a relay race. It was as if the man Jesus had been reproduced on the earth—ten, twenty, and soon a hundredfold. The new consciousness is no respecter of persons. All it needs is a human vessel that has been spiritually prepared and primed to receive it. This was definitely the case with the apostles. Their three years of intensive discipleship spent with Jesus almost guaranteed that they would receive the new consciousness for themselves.

It must also be noted that this was a particularly *anointed* timeframe and earthly location. This anointing was largely attributable to Jesus, who had just enacted the most powerful demonstration of the new consciousness ever witnessed among men. The light of Jesus' consciousness was so powerful that it left a kind of residual vacuum after he departed—a vacuum into which God's Spirit rushed, seeking expression in human vessels. The apostles that had been with Jesus were the first to receive the indwelling Spirit, but many others soon followed. Thus the new consciousness spread like wildfire for quite some time. Then mostly through the efforts of the Apostle Paul, it broke through the borders of Palestine and was introduced to the wide world, being revealed as the universal force it has always been.

Paul was also given the revelation that the apostolic commission need not be restricted to a chosen few. Neither did it need to be associated with particular criteria, such as being with Jesus or being a member of the first church. Thus it was Paul who redefined the term *apostle* and gave it more of a universal character. According to Pauline teaching, the criteria for being an apostle were primarily the spiritual attainment of God-realization and the developing of the consciousness of God union, and this state of enlightenment was proved not by human claims or associations but rather strictly by demonstration. This meant that the title *apostle* could now be bestowed upon any human being, regardless of gender, race, religious affiliation, or nationality. It was the indwelling Spirit and the degree of consciousness development that made one an apostle, not some human ability. It also meant that there was now no limit as to how many apostles might be alive on the earth at any given time.

Having many apostles upon the earth did not water down their authority. On the contrary, as long as their calling was genuine, it translated into a sort of heyday for the new consciousness. It made the demonstration of the Spirit's power more prolific than ever. It was like having Jesus' ministry pop up in every city of the western world at the same time. So the unique quality of this time in the unfoldment of spiritual consciousness cannot be overstated. In Paul's day and for several decades following his death there were literally scores of apostles actively ministering in the Mediterranean region, promoting the spread of the new consciousness in a way that had never been done before. The teaching of these apostles was highly authoritative, and their demonstration was with the power of signs and wonders.

Understandably, this was a bleak period for the proponents of the status quo. They had succeeded in silencing Jesus' testimony, but to their great consternation the testimony of the apostles turned out to be much more difficult to stamp out. All they could do was to lay low and hope that the spread of the new consciousness burned itself out at some point, as wildfires are wont to do when they run out of tinder. And this is precisely what happened, though it was several centuries before there was not a trace of it left.

The Teaching of the Apostles

As time passed and fewer and fewer genuine apostles could be found, the status quo seized the opportunity to regain control over human society and once again dictate the direction of human endeavor. Not only did they regain control; they also introduced many new forms of repression, indoctrination, and propaganda at this time with the aim of insuring that they would not have to suffer the ignominy and humiliation of watching the new consciousness proliferate again.

Thus the new consciousness was once again forced underground, while the apostolic age passed into oblivion. But this is not to imply that the fate of the new consciousness was now worse off than it had been before Jesus began his ministry. The world had seen a great light and had basked in that light for more than two centuries, thanks to the testimony of the apostles. Then even after the apostolic age ended, there remained a vestige of the light of spiritual truth that could not be destroyed. This vestige was mostly attributable to the teaching of the apostles—a teaching that had managed to elude the repressive tactics of the status quo.

The teaching of the apostles, as presented by those who had been with Jesus and by Paul, turned out to be vital to the future survival and leavening influence of the new consciousness. It was by no means a sophisticated or scholarly teaching, but it was wonderfully descriptive of the awe and wonder of God's active presence among men. This active presence was first manifested in their master Jesus. So, much of the apostles' teaching centers on an objective recanting of the life of Jesus and his works and sayings. "The law was given through Moses; grace and truth came through Jesus Christ," John wrote (John 1:17). And this comparison of two of Israel's most inspired spiritual leaders sets the tone for the apostolic teaching that was ultimately handed down to us. In other words, the teaching of the apostles, because of their faithful handling of Jesus' testimony, also became a vehicle for grace and truth.

But this teaching's perpetuation has not been without difficulties. Not only was it distorted and maligned by the status quo, but it also faced inbred hurdles. For one thing, our world has changed almost unrecognizably. Two thousand years have elapsed since the apostolic age. This has rendered the terminology and imagery used by the apostles as practically obsolete. Even the concepts of grace and truth have been largely obscured by modern human endeavor. So before we can fully understand all that the apostles were trying to impart, we must clear our minds of their modern cultural indoctrination and go back in time. We must be open to the possibility that behind their archaic language there are pearls of timeless universal truth and think for ourselves when it comes to the common belief that something so outdated cannot have any value.

The writings of the Apostle Paul pose the greatest challenge in this regard. The fact is that Paul, who was actually an erudite and scholarly man, employed terminology and imagery that most modern intellectuals tend to utterly reject as being both absurd and offensive. The reason for this is on account of Paul's orthodox religious background. While none of the apostles that had been with Jesus were particularly religious, Paul, on the other hand, was highly trained as a Jewish rabbi. Moreover, he never viewed it as imperative to forsake that training. Therefore content aside, the Pauline writings are in fact thoroughly Jewish in tone and terminology. It might even be said that the only thing that sets Christianity apart from Judaism is its doctrinal content. Without that distinction, it might very well be viewed as a sect or offshoot of Judaism.

It is this Jewish connection that causes modern intellectuals to recoil, primarily because Judaism has its roots in a pre-intellectual era. Christianity may be two thousand years old, but it is young in comparison to Judaism. It appeared on a world scene that was already reflecting the values of modern western society (during the height of the Roman empire). But Judaism was introduced into our world at a time when human life was still largely tribal and men's minds were steeped in heathenism and superstition. Judaism then belongs to an entirely different world, and its terminology and imagery are indeed archaic. But through Paul this archaic religion was revived and presented in such a convincing format that it ended up being adopted by the western world as its generic cultural-religious framework.

The other apostles may not have been religiously orthodox, but they were nonetheless Jews in the cultural sense. So they too tended to inculcate the basic tenets of the faith of their forefathers. They clearly valued their heritage and saw no reason to reject it entirely. In fact, among all the apostles the common view was that the newly emerging religion called Christianity was not to be thought of as separate or independent at all. It was to be seen as a continuation or expanded revelation of that original western spiritual blueprint called Judaism.

Thus we find that the religious aspect of culture we have been raised in here in the west is in fact essentially Judeo-Christian. It is a mix of Jewish law and values with the doctrine of messianic salvation added on as a sort of revelatory amendment. The only real exception to this general apostolic impartation is the writing of the Apostle John, which though also Jewish in terminology and imagery, presents a more universal, impersonal, and therefore purely spiritual viewpoint. In this sense John's testimony was the most closely aligned with Jesus' own.

As a whole, however, it must be understood that in terms of consciousness expansion the teaching of the apostles has been anything but a dynamo. It was far from being a clear and cogent disputation of the new consciousness. Rather it was more of an Adamic mindset with some new religious doctrines to mull over thrown in. This ought not to surprise us, because it is entirely possible to be Adamic in our general orientation and devout in our religious inclinations. Religious devotion does not necessarily bring about a change in consciousness, because it usually maintains a distance between man and God. Only the revelation of messianic redemption and reconciliation, which is not religious at all, develops our consciousness by breaking down all the engrained barriers.

When our view of God is as a separate, distant, unapproachable being, it is very easy to entertain false notions about God's nature. This has been the problem for the Jewish people throughout their religious history. Being influenced by their heathen neighbors and civilizations, the Jews often veered off into a form of worship that was both superstitious and fearful. The revolutionary teaching of God's true nature as *One God* given to them by Moses ultimately became distorted and diluted. The law was preserved, but the Spirit was neglected. The Jewish concept of God was as a demanding, capricious tyrant, impossible to please and ready to exercise vengeance on His disobedient people at the drop of a hat. It was through this false concept that a whole new terminology emerged—words like *sin, damnation, purgatory, divine judgment, and condemnation*. To *fear* God was considered the highest wisdom. Unfortunately, this conceptual worship and fear-based terminology was carried over into Christianity, and the vehicle for this transference was none other than the teaching of the apostles.

Thus the teaching of the apostles might be viewed as both a failure and a success. It failed to present the Gospel of Jesus as a streamlined universal truth, which when acting upon human consciousness can lift us out of the degradation of the Adam mind. But it succeeded in keeping the testimony of the new consciousness alive and thriving. In fact, it might even be said that it was the apostles' testimony handed down through the writings of the New Testament that caused the potentiality of the new consciousness to be interwoven into western civilization in such a way that it could never again be extinguished by the status quo's agenda.

The apostles' failure stemmed from their own lack of conscious awareness. On account of their time spent with Jesus and their experience of the Spirit's indwelling presence on the day of Pentecost, they could instinctually live the Spirit-led life of the new consciousness. But they were unable to impart the liberating spiritual principles to others, as Jesus had done. Thus they themselves never attained master status. Rather their testimony was based more on who they were and how they lived than what they taught in words.

The New Consciousness Breaks Free

Unfortunately, the religious tone of the apostles' teaching has had a detrimental effect on the spread of the new consciousness in the collective psyche. It might even be said that this one weakness in their testimony has delayed the eventual and inevitable spiritual enlightenment of our species. To box up the messianic revelation of God union in a religious framework robbed it of much of its inherent power. For, once it was neatly packaged in this form, it made the individual acceptance of the new consciousness dependent upon the embracing of the religion that housed it. This was fine for those for whom religion is a good fit, but it tended to repel those who have no affinity for organized spirituality.

It is also entirely plausible that the proponents of the status quo had a hand in this religious coup. Since it has always been their agenda to render the new consciousness as anemic as possible, they might very well have seized the opportunity to associate the streamlined spiritual testimony of Jesus with Judeo-Christian theology. But if such was indeed the case, it was the religious tone of the teaching of the apostles that rendered such an association as fluid and natural.

The good news is that the new consciousness is such a dynamic and expansive force that it cannot be boxed up forever, whether in a religious framework or any other conceptual house. Its light is too strong, as has been seen at other stages of our collective consciousness development. Even being linked to the Church's blood lust and oppression of the poor has not tarnished the pure essence of spiritual consciousness. Now what we are witnessing in our time is the breaking free of the new consciousness from its religious association and the establishing of it as a universal current of indestructible life. We see the testimony of Jesus having revived as a non-religious phenomenon. We also see the testimony of the apostles slipping into oblivion.

The reason for this shift in the collective psyche away from religion and toward a universal timeless spirituality is attributable to the age-long progression toward enlightenment and away from fear and narrow mindedness. Jesus was a prophet and as such could see far into the future. He saw the age of religion playing itself out and ultimately coming to an end, and he knew that the new consciousness was no passing phase, but rather would endure unto eternity. Thus he kept the teaching of it free and pure.

How do we know that the time for the new consciousness has finally arrived? For one thing, the status quo in our day is no longer the diligent repressive power it once was. Perhaps due to complacency, it has relaxed its grip on human society and allowed tolerance and universalism to gain a solid foothold. It is true that the culture of man has become so thoroughly conditioned and secularized that most people still view spiritual consciousness as just another anemic religious alternative. But it is precisely this development that has caused the status quo to become complacent and lose its edge.

When seen in the perspective of human history's woeful saga, this day has certainly been long overdue. The price of the collective enlightenment of our species has been paid in much blood. All of the apostles were martyred, as were all who carried the torch of the new consciousness after them. But now for us, martyrdom is no longer inescapable. In the privacy of our own homes we can pursue consciousness development without fearing for our lives. And our progress in this pursuit will continue to go unhindered.

The age-old enmity of Cain against his brother Abel has at long last simmered out. Now is the time for us to wake up from the prodigal dream of Adam and lay hold of the divine inheritance that our Father has been keeping for us.

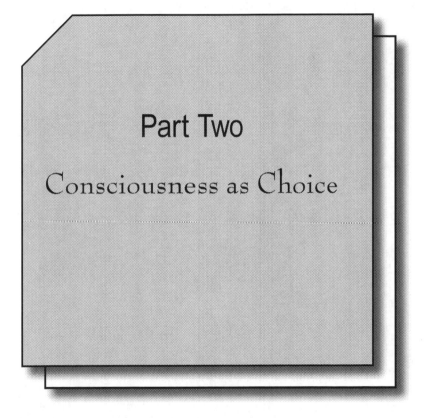

Part Two

Consciousness as Choice

Chapter Five

Yes and No

For us in this modern era who are pursuing enlightenment through the new consciousness, it still behooves us to keep our spiritual bent private and quiet. No one is going to bother us, if we keep to ourselves. The status quo will not go out of its way to persecute us anymore. Nevertheless, if we are wise, we will establish and maintain our inner world as a spiritual sanctuary—a place that is inviolably under the sovereign rule of God's Spirit. The degree to which we are able to do this will factor into our progress. Up until now we have in all likelihood been zealous to change the world, but now our focus must shift. Now we must leave the world to its own destiny and secure our own liberation as a top priority. This shift in priorities is described in the New Testament in these words: "Save yourself from this corrupt generation." (Acts 2:40). If each one of us individually raises his or her state of consciousness to that of God union, we can be sure that we will then be living in a changed world.

Our only concern then becomes our inner world. We do not even concern ourselves any longer with our life's circumstances and outward situation. True, it is expedient to get this aspect of things running smoothly enough that it commands as little attention as possible, but once this is accomplished we no longer need to pay it any mind. The new consciousness is a strictly inward pursuit. Thus our object becomes to familiarize ourselves more and more with this previously neglected realm. As we do this we begin to perceive the mystical quality of the human psyche. The more conscious awareness we focus on it, the more we gain the revelation of just how vast and expansive a realm it is.

The kingdom of God is within us. This means the entire spiritual creation—a vast infinite universe beyond the scope of our human mind's comprehension. Our inner realm is also timeless and eternal. It was extant prior to our birth and will be extant after our death. Thus aligning ourselves with this inner kingdom through the new consciousness of reconciliation with God brings us into harmony with this infinite eternal life.

Our true eternal identity thrives in God's kingdom—that is, our inner sanctified landscape. Therefore as we pursue the new consciousness and seek to become more and more familiar with our inner world, we are in essence changing addresses—from this temporal world of men to the eternal kingdom of God. For many this seems like a daunting shift, but in truth it is not difficult for us. Rather it is our natural estate. It is a lot like coming home therefore.

Changing addresses then is our starting point. It is like arriving at a new travel destination. We take a look around, see how life functions here, and open ourselves to the gradual pursuit of getting acclimated. Perhaps we might feel a little uncomfortable at first with the foreign aspect of being in a new place. But as we become acclimated we begin to relax. And as we relax and our mind becomes calmer, we are then able to make clear-minded assessments of what we are perceiving. We are able to become conscious of thoughts and feelings that were previously unconscious. We recognize that some of these thoughts and emotions are actually *patterns* that we have rehearsed over and over, without being aware that that was what we were doing. They are set off by certain *triggers* in the outer circumstantial realm and are therefore *reactionary*.

This awareness is actually our individual consciousness beginning to stir and develop. In the beginning stages these forays into consciousness tend to have two distinct qualities: there is the awareness of where *we presently are* in our consciousness and the awareness of where we *aspire to be*. We understand that these are inward realities only and that no one else can see what we are seeing about ourselves. Therefore we can be completely honest in this realm and not pretend we are someplace we are not.

Generally speaking, our consciousness tends to be severely underdeveloped at this stage. This is because we have neglected our inner world for most of our lives and carried on in an unconscious mode. So when we measure the state we are presently in against the state we aspire to be in, the distance may seem formidable. But consciousness development can be full of surprises. That great distance we perceive can be traversed in the blink of an eye. Progress in the spiritual life comes via revelation and realization, not necessarily through a long drawn out evolutionary unfoldment. Consciousness does not learn like the human mind does; it recognizes truth and responds. The problem is that we have been thoroughly conditioned to believe in non-truths. Therefore for most of us to make progress in the realm of consciousness development, there must first be a process of *unlearning*. And it is this process that takes time and makes that distance between where we are now and where we want to get to seem long indeed.

This initial acclimation to our inner world with its honest assessments, hopes, and seeming impediments is a universal spiritual experience, shared by all who are becoming conscious. In our parabolic literature we find that this was Adam's predicament in the garden. He too perceived consciousness in terms of choice. In fact, it might even be said that the time frame of the parable coincided with Adam's readiness to choose—a readiness that we all eventually arrive at. In other words, the garden experience manifested in Adam's life as the result of his inward directive. This means that each one of us at this stage in our spiritual development figuratively also enters the garden in order to make the same choice that Adam was confronted with. The only difference is that our choice involves a state of consciousness that has now been in prominent usage for over six thousand years, while Adam's choice was between two states of consciousness that were both new to him. This has lent a clarity to our choice that Adam did not have. Like Adam, we are confronted with the same two states of consciousness to choose between, but unlike Adam, we have a good deal of evidence and testimony concerning the state that we have now come to associate with Adam's choice—the state that we call Adamic consciousness. Therefore our choice is whether to continue in the Adamic mode of duality and willful prodigality or to go higher toward the state of full God union and realization. We also have a much better understanding of the repercussions and ramifications of our choice than Adam had. All he knew was that the knowledge of good and evil would eventually lead to death. But we have had six thousand years of actual demonstration to illuminate the situation. We have all seen what Adamic consciousness does. We have all experienced its plagues and devastations. And we know that death is not to be toyed with, but rather avoided at all costs.

Our choice then is between these two states of consciousness only: the state of Adamic duality and prodigality and the state of full reconciliation with God or realized God union. It is not an option for us to choose both; neither is it an option to sit on the fence and not choose at all. Rather there comes a time in every human being's experience when he or she *must* choose, even if that time may not be in this lifetime. Whether in this lifetime or a later one, the choice will wait for us, however. Thus it behooves us to prepare ourselves and approach that day with full cognizance and responsibility. For, the consequences we set in motion can be dire.

As human beings, it is up to us then to decide which way we will go. There is in actuality nothing acting upon us from outside of ourselves to influence this decision. Neither can there be any real progress in consciousness development, until the choice for God realization is made. That is why the Parable of the Garden was placed at the beginning of the Bible. The fact that Adam chose to reject the new consciousness at the dawn of human civilization has been shown to be the root cause for everything that has followed—that is, human history. The binding negative repercussions of his choice have plagued our species throughout this age. The darkness of ignorance and superstition has resulted in unfathomable suffering for our species. And yet, it is not too late to turn things around.

Saying **No** *to Adam*

Perhaps the greatest miracle of divine intervention in this age of man is the fact that we still have a choice. This is not to say that the status quo movement has not tried to conceal and deny this. It has taught that Adam's choice was binding for our collective destiny and has sought to perpetuate the reign of Adamic consciousness indefinitely. It has actively resisted and maligned the very idea that there is such a thing as an alternative consciousness. It has developed a highly sophisticated subjective reality system in order to effectually insure that Adamic consciousness never passes away. And yet, because this is God's universe and not man's, a choice still remains.

The fact is that not only is the choice still there for the making, but ever since Jesus came and testified concerning the new consciousness the argument against Adam has been gaining momentum. This means that as each one of us enters the garden and is confronted with Adam's choice, we now have the light of Jesus' teaching to illuminate our decision as well as six thousand years worth of evidence against making the same mistake Adam made. We are therefore in no way bound to follow in Adam's footsteps.

In light of these present day dynamics, the choice before us actually becomes a relatively easy one, and many of us find as we turn inward for the first time that we are ready to say *yes* to the new consciousness. Having discovered this potentiality within our own being, we feel empowered by these developments and begin to envision a future with God consciousness as the governing consciousness of human society.

Our primary difficulty, as it turns out, comes when we are confronted with the Adam mind's reluctance to give way and relinquish its control over us. Saying *yes* to the new consciousness is one thing, but actually implementing the changes that such a choice requires is another. Thus we must be prepared for the Adam mind to wage a war of doubt and fear to try to persuade us to continue with the status quo. But there is a method for facilitating the transition that the Adam mind is not prepared for. This method involves simply exerting our God-given authority and putting the Adam mind in its rightful place. Practically speaking, in the same way we say *yes* to the new consciousness, we say *no* to Adam—a *no* that is conscious, assertive, and persistent.

It is not that the Adam mind holds any appeal for us anymore. We have seen and experienced its devastations often enough to be convinced that its time is over. But the need to consciously disavow and disassociate ourselves from Adam soon becomes apparent, when we understand that one of the Adam mind's best weapons is unconsciousness. We come to realize this by a simple process of observing our mental and emotional activity. And what we see may be a little shocking. As it turns out, we are actually unconscious more often than we are conscious. Then to rub it in, we find that whenever we are unconscious we are really *in Adam*. In other words, unconsciousness is just another facet of Adamic consciousness.

Unconsciousness is not to be confused with nothingness or a blank, vegetative state. On the contrary, unconsciousness invariably involves thinking and emoting. But this thinking and emoting is carried out automatically, without observation from our higher Self. It is this lack of awareness that renders it as unconsciousness—not the absence of mental activity. Only as we become aware of this unconscious mind activity, do we come to realize that unconsciousness is really just the Adam mind running amok. In other words, unconsciousness is a signal that the Adam mind is firmly in control. Therefore when we make the decision to say *no* to Adam, we must not forget to extend that *no* to unconscious thinking and emoting. These tend to pass themselves off as harmless and even playful, but they are in reality just as detrimental to us as any other aspect of Adamic consciousness.

Is unconsciousness always Adamic? Yes. This is because of our infantile conditioning. Ever since human culture came to uphold and reflect the Adam mind, we have all been born into the choice of Adam and remain in that condition until such time as we become mature enough to choose and think for ourselves. Thus our indulgence in unconscious thought and emotion is really just a conditioned reflex. Psychologically, we have become clones of Adam and one another, and whenever we lapse into unconsciousness this cloned conditioned mind holds sway. In fact, that is one of the main causes for unconsciousness. Essentially, we have become so disinterested and bored with the entire conditioned mindset of Adam that we tune it out and let it run automatically.

Nevertheless, when seeking to reverse the Adam mentality and its lifelong devastations, we must make the unconscious conscious, see it for what it truly is, and consciously reject it for ourselves. This will make our *no* a thorough and complete one, without leaving behind any hidden pockets of Adamic consciousness that can crop up and trouble us later.

We must make it our goal to utterly eradicate all traces of darkened Adamic consciousness, and we do this through the light of our own awareness. To be diligent in this matter makes our choice impregnable. To constantly call to mind the devastations of the Adamic orientation is to set our feet firmly on the path of the new consciousness.

The devastations of the Adam mind are no secret. They have been the cause of most of our personal problems as well as the bane of human society in general. But we have been so propagandized and conditioned that we have become largely desensitized to our suffering. We have come to view these terrible devastations as simply an inescapable aspect of human life. We have accepted the inevitability of death and come to believe that disease, sin, lack, and limitation are normal human conditions. We have not understood that these are the results or *demonstration* of Adamic consciousness and are therefore subject to our own choice. We were never taught that we have the power to say *no* to Adam.

As we progress in this program of the authoritative dismissal of the Adam mind, we find that we are dealing increasingly with unconsciousness. This is because it does not take long to recognize the devastations of Adamic consciousness and begin addressing them. When we realize that there is no good that can come from the Adam mind controlling our inner world, saying *no* to Adam becomes a sane and reasonable response. But then little by little as we become aware of how often we lapse into unconsciousness and see that this unconsciousness is really just another facet of Adamic consciousness, we realize that we still have plenty of work to do. The program is the same, with the exception that we must now first bring each unconscious thought and emotion into the light of awareness before we can say *no* to it. And this takes time.

Dealing with unconsciousness can be a little tricky too. Thought and emotion are often intricately interwoven. Deciphering which is which and what is the source of our current devastation can be difficult sometimes. Triggers set us off and cause us to react before we can gain any awareness of what is happening. And circumstances tend to pile on and add a sense of urgency to our predicament. Thus it is not uncommon for even a spiritually attuned individual to get lost in an unconscious train for a while. In the end, however, the light of awareness always prevails. Once we stop and take the time to focus, the utter insubstantial quality of our unconsciousness is exposed and banished.

Saying Yes to the New Consciousness

Saying *yes* to the new consciousness may seem like an obvious and redundant thing to do, but in actuality it is a very important activity that empowers us to make fast and sure progress on the spiritual path. Moreover, it is an activity that bespeaks an already highly developed state of spiritual consciousness.

The new consciousness is the consciousness of God union. It is the unwavering realization that God is present in our inner world at all times and regardless of where our body may be. And it is the initiative of saying *yes* to that presence that activates its power. In other words, it is our *yes* that releases the presence to do what it does—that is, to bring forth the benign demonstration of God's power.

The difficulty is that in order for our *yes* to activate God's presence in our inner world, we must first be fully convinced that God's Spirit resides therein. This full conviction cannot be faked. In a sense it must be earned—earned through long hours of quiet contemplation and logical deduction. It is the full fruit of the teaching of Jesus and the New Testament doctrine of messianic redemption. It is not a religious matter, but it *is* an attained state of spiritual consciousness. It is therefore a requirement, the likes of which there can be no sidestepping.

Another curious aspect of this dynamic is the role of our own conscious awareness in activating God's power. Even after we are fully convinced that God's Spirit dwells within us, it may seem strange to us that our own conscious *yes* acts like a switch to unleash that Spirit's power. But such is the case. It is as if God desired there to be a cosmic cooperation between Itself and man, and without participating in this cooperative dance there will be no power and no demonstration. It is surprising how many sincere spiritual aspirants are in the dark about this particular mechanism. They have come to believe that God's Spirit is present within them, but out of a kind of false humility they cannot imagine that their own cooperation or conscious *yes* would play a part in the divine operative. And so *the presence* lingers and languishes in inactivity.

Saying *yes* then to the new consciousness is not just a spiritual discipline or exercise. It is an integral key to becoming a participant in the demonstration of God's power. Therefore let us examine this *yes* a little closer. It goes without saying that when we say *yes*, we are not just mouthing the word or reciting some formulated incantation. How then ought our *yes* to be?

First, we must get still. Saying *yes* to God is a holy interaction that requires concentration and a meditative approach. We cannot very well say *yes* to God's activity while simultaneously occupying ourselves with some other project. Such a *yes* will invariably be insincere and manipulative and therefore pagan. In other words, the pagans of old believed that certain words or phrases unlocked God's power. Thus they employed formulated verbal incantations strictly for the purpose of getting God to support their own human agenda. This must never be our approach. We must never seek to use God to further our own agenda. Rather we say *yes* to God's activity in our inner world for the furtherance of God's kingdom on earth. That is why quiet meditation is called for. We must take the time to make sure our motives are pure. We must be dedicated to the prayer: "Thy kingdom come on earth as it is in heaven."

We begin our meditation with the affirmation: *I am here, now*. This banishes all unconsciousness and helps us to focus on the present moment. But again we do not merely recite these words; we *feel* them until we know that we are fully there. Only when we are fully present in the moment will our *yes* be pure and non-manipulative.

We follow this by consciously acknowledging God's presence. We might say the words: *God is here.* This is a profound truth that bears constant recollection. It might very well evoke in our minds the teaching of the New Testament—that is, that I have been reconciled to God through Christ and Jesus' assurance to the apostles that God would send *the Counselor* to them after Jesus was no longer with them in the flesh (John 16:7). This idea that God dwells in us by Its Spirit may seem fantastic, but it is the truth. It is also a powerful antidote to unconsciousness. As a matter of fact, consciously knowing that we are in God's presence often clicks us into a kind of super-conscious state—that is, a state wherein every thought and emotion that is not of God is immediately exposed and rejected. When this happens to us, our consciousness has not only become present and active; it has also become purified and sanctified. This state of super-consciousness is the realization that since God is present within us and God is holy, the ground whereupon I stand is also holy.

Now we are ready to unleash God's activity and power. We have said *yes* to the consciousness of God's presence, and behold God's power begins to sweep through our inner world. This is another reason for being in a meditative state. When God begins to move inside of us, the last thing we want is to be physically or mentally distracted or preoccupied. We will want to give the divine impetus our full attention and conscious assent.

As we consciously abide with God's active presence, the result is a scientifically predictable demonstration of spiritual power. This power may manifest as bodily healing, moral strength, financial increase, or just a sense of cleanness and overall well-being. When God is released to be God, God will surely do all that is in Its nature to do. In this way our inner landscape gradually becomes transformed, and when our inner world comes to reflect God's glory it will not be long before our outer circumstances also align thusly.

Chapter Six

The Four Doors

The general principle of the new consciousness is that God's Spirit dwells within us *and* that God's beneficent scientifically consistent activity can be unleashed therein by our conscious *yes* or cooperative conscious realization. This is the fulfillment of the Gospel of Jesus the Christ, who promised just such an outpouring to his disciples prior to his crucifixion.

Thus through this amazing spiritual dynamic we become partakers in the divine life. We also are empowered to reverse all the harmful devastations of the Adam mind—devastations that have plagued humanity since at least the beginning of the modern era. This reversal in men's fortunes has been referred to in many ways. Some have called it salvation; some have likened it to a new birth or life from the dead; some have focused on its healing aspect; some have viewed it as the key to prosperity, and others have brought it under the one doctrinal heading: redemption. In truth, it is all these things. This is because there is really only one solution for the many and varied problems of human existence: the activity of God.

The activity of God in our inner world is all we need, because when that realm is healed and swept clean, our outer circumstances soon reflect this by becoming orderly, sane, and problem-free. Indeed the entire discordant tone of human life as we have known it disappears. So, in truth, we no longer need to pay attention to the outer sphere. We only need to focus on the inward dynamic.

This same truth applies to the devastations of the Adam mind. All outward manifestations have an inward basis. Therefore though we once believed that our problems happened *to us*, having their source in some outward environmental or circumstantial effect, in actuality their cause was invariably inward, arising from the Adamic state of consciousness.

What all this adds up to is a new recognition of just how crucial our inner world's climate and activity are. It is this inward condition that determines the fruit of our lives, and it is by our fruit that we are known. Consciousness, whether it be of the Adam mind or of the presence of God's Spirit, acts upon us to either bear good fruit or discord and death.

The new consciousness is the consciousness of God's presence unleashing God's activity in our inner world. As such, when it arises, it automatically banishes the unconscious Adam mind activity that had been controlling us up to that point. Human beings cannot have two such divergent states of consciousness acting upon them at the same time. What we *can* do is to discern whether and when we are being acted upon by Adamic consciousness and change that direction in mid-stream. This discernment becomes relatively easy, when we learn which fruits to associate with the Adam mind. These fruits are a scientific certainty, so we need not fear being tricked or deceived by them. In other words, in the same way that we have learned not to expect to find ripe juicy apples growing on a thorn bush, we can learn not to expect the Adam mind to produce harmonious conditions. Just as reaching out and touching a thorn bush causes bleeding fingers, indulging Adamic consciousness always yields devastation.

Being able to discern between the fruits of these two states of consciousness also helps us to choose between them with full cognizance and conviction. It makes our *yes* to the new consciousness a vibrant and faithful one and our *no* to the Adam mind unwavering and authoritative.

As a kind of overall benefit, any new awareness we gain concerning the workings of our inner realm strengthens us in the truth. It is no secret that the level of inner awareness for most modern Westerners is very low. This is because our culture has placed very little value on gaining such awareness and has instead promoted the idea that we have no need whatsoever to know the truth about what is going on inside of us. Ours is a culture of escapism and distraction, not inner awareness. In fact, most of us have gotten so out of touch with our inner workings that our condition is really one of self-estrangement. We may be materialistically fulfilled and intellectually stimulated, but when it comes to knowing ourselves we are completely clueless.

So as we begin our inward journey we may feel like we are groping in the dark. It is a little like being in a dark hallway and looking for a door that, when opened, will cause light to shine in. Luckily, the inner world of a human being is so expansive that there are actually four such doors, with each one opening into a distinct branch or field of inner reality. As we open each one of these doors we find it bathed in a powerful light, and that light exposes the truth about that particular aspect of our inner world. For example, behind the door of the supply register we are shown whether we are receiving our supply by the divine law of grace or fighting for it by the sweat of our brow. We are shown whether we are enjoying God's inexhaustible abundance or suffering from the plague of lack and limitation. And so by opening each of these four doors and looking within we can essentially learn the complete and true condition of our inner world. Basically, we will find one of two sets of conditions in operation: the good fruit and benign demonstration of the new consciousness or the devastations of the Adam mind.

There is no great mystery about this. If when we open one of our four doors of perception, we find devastation of any form or kind, we can be sure that the Adam mind has been having its way with us. Conversely, if we have begun saying *yes* to the new consciousness of God's presence and activity, we will find goodness and healing. And so little by little, our inner world becomes known and familiar to us. We not only begin to understand the cause and effects associated with these two powerful states of consciousness, but we also gain honest insight into our own degree of spiritual progress.

Consistency and predictability are the tenets of science. Behind our four doors we will find scientifically reliable evidence of our inner condition. Behind the first door or life register we will gain a glimpse into our true aliveness or lack of it. Behind our second door or body register we will see to what degree our consciousness is impacting our health. Behind our third door or supply register we will learn the difference between being supplied by grace and the approach of the world in going after existing supply. And behind our fourth door or soul register we will behold the effects of the terrible plague of sin and the amazing ministry of God's redemptive principle.

The four doors then effectually give us a good start in the pursuit of self-knowledge. To see and acknowledge the effects of consciousness acting upon these four crucial aspects of the human experience is to understand some of the hidden laws of creation as they pertain to man. These laws of creation are binding upon our experience. Therefore it behooves us to learn of them and in learning, to arrive at a place of submission and peace about them. Though the inner workings of man can seem daunting and complex, in truth, once we understand the laws and spiritual principles that act upon us, the picture becomes greatly simplified. A perfect example of this is the realization that we are acted upon by consciousness, not just inwardly but outwardly and circumstantially as well. Just this one realization can shed tremendous light on the human predicament. But enlightenment does not stop there. We can and must learn every angle of what makes us tick. We can and must stop hiding from ourselves and taking refuge in every form of escape, diversion, and distraction that our culture dangles before us. True life is never unconscious. It is never a groping in the dark. Knowledge brings light, and knowledge of our own inner workings brings en *light* enment.

The Life Register

Behind each of our four doors we will find that one of two states of consciousness has been dominant and holding sway: either the Adamic state of duality and prodigality or the consciousness of God's presence and activity. We can also interact with both the prevailing state of consciousness and its demonstration. In other words, if we are being confronted with the devastations of the Adam mind, it is within our power to change that demonstration by our *yes* or *no*. We can decide whether to continue on in the devastation or put an end to it. Therefore our presence is both observant *and* interactive. This is a truly wonderful capability, as we will soon discover.

For the sake of understanding then, I will enter each door and describe what I see from the perspective of one entering that door in his or her inner world for the first time. The reason for this is that it is almost a given that as a first time participant we all will confront the devastations of the Adam mind, pretty much across the board. This will help us to be able to recognize these devastations, as well as learn the correct methodology for positive interaction.

The first door or life register is actually like a control room, where we can view our life levels as they pertain to our inner world. Remember that this is not taking into account our outward attempts to mask who we really are. Rather it is a *true* reading of life levels that reveals the *true* condition of our inner world. So get ready for a shock.

If we are moving in and being acted upon by Adamic consciousness, as the vast majority of people are, the first thing that will hit us is not the high levels of life found behind this door; it is the appalling dearth of life. In other words, the inward life levels of most modern Westerners are, as a rule, dangerously low. They are so low that they are more reflective of death than life. Therefore the first devastation of the Adam mind that we encounter is the devastation of death.

What is the appearance of death? Imagine a stark desert landscape, where the climatic conditions are so severe that nothing can grow. The ground is like flint; the air is dry and cold, and the out picturing is one of emptiness, barrenness, and lifelessness. Another image is that of the proverbial *hard heart*—that is, the heart that is completely unresponsive to life and love. This is the condition of our life levels when acted upon by the prodigal-Adam mind. This mind sees itself as being cut off from God, which means that any life that comes from God is off limits to us. And contrary to modern belief, human beings have no true life of their own. Therefore most of us, regardless of the image we give off to the world, live our lives void of life. We eek out our projected lifespan of seventy or eighty years by drawing on our natural given strength, until that strength gives out. But that strength is not true life. That is why it cannot be replenished and invariably ends in death.

There is no human solution to the devastation of death. Science cannot help us here. Since death has come into our experience as the result of Adamic consciousness, the only solution is a change of consciousness. True, we can aspire to nobly accept the inevitability of death, and that is what our culture teaches us to do. But this acceptance in no way removes death's scourge. The sting of human death is unparalleled in all the rest of creation. All created forms die, but they do so in the vein of changing forms. There is no cessation of life, no fear, and no resistance, such as we experience. There is only the reconstituting of indestructible life. Thus we come to understand that human death is unnatural. It comes out of an unnatural disturbed mindset, and its presence in our inner world wreaks havoc upon us as a devastation.

What we find inside this first door then is the effect of human death upon our inner world. It is death at work in us, even while we are still alive in the body. And if we do not experience a change of consciousness, death will continue to have its way with us until eventually our bodies reflect the inner reality and succumb to the grave. But the good news is that through a change in consciousness—through embracing and abiding in the new consciousness—we can and will vanquish death, first in its present inward demonstration and then subsequently in its formerly inescapable outward manifestation.

This shift in consciousness is within our grasp at any time, but it must be undertaken with full awareness and responsibility. First, we must honestly assess the many ways that the devastation of human death has been actively having its way with us. Then we must say *no* to that devastation and *yes* to the presence and activity of God's Spirit. As soon as we are able to do this, we will experience the reversal of the devastation of death or that which the New Testament calls *resurrection life.*

The moment we say *yes* to the new consciousness, new life begins to course through our inner world. And this is now God's life, which means that it is life eternal and indestructible. It is the same life that animates all created life—the life that causes plants to flower and bear fruit. It is the life of God's fruitfulness.

In the Bible this life is likened to streams of living water (Isaiah 35:6). As these streams flow into our barren landscape, they moisten, soften, and saturate. They break up the fallow ground. They fill all the cold empty places. They make our heart pliable and capable of love. They make us receptive to God's voice and will. In short, they change our demonstration from death to life.

Thus we come to see how Adamic consciousness brings the devastation of death into our experience and how for most people that devastation not only steers us inexorably toward the grave; it also greatly impacts our life. It is this devastation that causes us to demonstrate desperate and tragic conditions in our outward life situation. The emptiness inside of us reflects outwardly as discord, disharmony, and suffering. It gives rise to the Darwinian prodigal orientation that causes us to strive, fight, and connive to make our way. Then after acting out death's demonstration in our lifetime, we fluidly accept as inevitable its demonstration at the grave.

It does not take inordinate discernment to see that our present human culture is a death-obsessed one. The reason for this can be traced directly to the workings of each individual's inner realm. Behind each one's first door are devastatingly low life readings that do not lie. These individual low life levels have given rise to a collective mindset that is so crippled by the fear of death that it can hardly be called life anymore.

We go through life pretending. We think that if we adopt a grateful attitude just to have seventy or eighty years of life between the cradle and the grave that we are doing well. But such an attitude does not get to the root of the problem. Only when we stop running from ourselves and turn inward will we begin to move towards a real solution. Only when each one of us looks inside that first door and beholds the desert of devastation therein will we begin to reverse our cultural death obsession. And only through our own interactive *yes* to God's presence and activity in the new consciousness can we cross that great divide from death to life (John 5:24).

The Body Register

Before we look inside our second door, called the *Body Register*, there are some cultural misconceptions about the human body that we must address and correct. Among these misconceptions is the idea that the body has a will and intelligence of its own and therefore acts independently as a physical entity.

The idea of the body acting independently according to its own agenda has no logical or scientific basis. Any scientist that has studied the workings of the body soon comes to the conclusion that the matter and organic activity that comprise the body have no inherent intelligence. True, the body will function automatically if left to itself, but whenever there is a change or digression from this involuntary activity it is always brought about, not by the body's own initiative, but rather by some outside influence *acting upon* the body—an influence that has at least some semblance of intelligence.

The problem is that while we revere scientific process in our culture, many of us do not think with the clarity and level-headedness of a scientist. Most of us, in fact, think rather irrationally, according to a belief system that is more superstitious and emotional than logical or empirical. This is especially true when it comes to bodily dysfunction. For, when we are in pain and the fear of death is upon us we tend to want to blame someone or something. This is how the idea that the body acts independently gained momentum in our culture. We see the body as a separate entity and most often, because it causes us pain, we see it as our enemy. We say, "I [meaning my body] caught a cold" or fell prey to contagion. When we get injured, we think that it happened because our body was not paying attention or was out-of-shape. We sometimes even succumb to the belief that our body manifests disease or injury just to spite us, because it wants to do us harm or is bent on destroying us.

But it is hardly possible for our body to be our enemy, when it has no intelligence of its own. Without its own intelligence, it can have neither intent nor agenda. It certainly cannot do anything out of spite or a destructive impulse. It cannot do anything other than function as a physical body. No, when our body becomes dysfunctional, it is not because of any will or impulse of its own. It is because something has *acted upon it*. Therefore the first step in approaching this second door is to stop blaming the body for causing us problems. The body is a lump of clay. Things act upon that clay to shape and govern it, but in itself it can do nothing.

The question then becomes: what is the primary force that acts upon the human body, thereby producing either optimal health or something less than optimal health? As we consider this question, at first it might occur to us that environmental causes fit the bill. For, clearly the environment acts upon the body in many ways. Do we not often say when not feeling well, "I'm feeling *under the weather?*" And if it is not the weather, it is the dampness, or pollution, or air-borne germs. Attributing poor health to environmental causes can even be proved scientifically, but this does not mean that environment is the primary causal force. The reason we know this is that not all bodies are susceptible to or negatively impacted by environmental influences. Some, in fact, are not affected in the least. Nevertheless, to attribute bodily conditions to environmental causes is definitely more scientific than to believe that the body is acting willfully out of spite. So it is a step in the right direction. But there must be something more.

The relatively new science of psychology has made a strong case for the claim that it is our mind that acts upon our body for good or evil. In this scenario, when our mind is sane, calm, lucid, and healthy, our body will reflect those qualities by functioning optimally and repelling negative environmental influences. On the contrary, if the mind is unsound and troubled, this also will be reflected in the body through weakness, dysfunction, and disease. Other scientists have given this psychological formula their approval, so that for those who are able to move beyond raw emotionalism and superstition, this has become the prevailing cultural belief. Indeed most modern Western intellectuals have now come to look at things this way—that is, that the body is acted upon primarily by the mind. This has dramatically altered the way we view disease and even death by rendering the pursuit of integral well being strictly a matter of mind. However, as foolproof as this formula seems to be, it is still not the primary force that acts upon the human body. There is yet a higher truth as it pertains to the body, and that truth involves spiritual consciousness. It is this truth that we encounter when we enter our second door. Here we find that it is our state of consciousness that acts upon our body and determines its condition.

How does spiritual consciousness differ from mind? The answer to this question hinges on that volatile word: *truth*. Spiritual consciousness reveals whether we are living in harmony with truth or in opposition to it. Or to put it another way, spiritual consciousness reveals whether we are in harmony with the creative principle as it pertains to our kind. What this means is that there can be no greater influence on the human psyche than spiritual consciousness. Mind may indeed act upon body, but spiritual consciousness acts upon the entire human psyche, including the mind. Therefore it is really spiritual consciousness that is the primary causal force acting upon the body.

Spiritual consciousness not only governs our inward human reality; it is the creative principle that determines all human function and demonstration. It is consciousness that created both our mind and body and therefore holds the blueprint for their optimal functioning. Therefore if there are problems in an individual human life experience, their source is always in consciousness. It also means that Adamic consciousness is holding sway. That is why the new consciousness is the all-encompassing solution to the present plight of humanity. Spiritual consciousness, or God, created us, and only a return to the governance of that original creative blueprint in our inner world can bring about the flourishing we yearn for. Changing our mind might have a minimal effect on our health, but only a change in consciousness can heal us and restore us to the perfection of being—a condition that greatly transcends mind.

As we enter the second door then—the door of the body register—we find the terrible devastation of disease at work, and we realize that this devastation has its source in consciousness. It may seem that the ailments from which our body suffers have their cause in environment or mind, but underlying that superficial assessment we understand that our body's malaise is deeper than it appears.

What is the body? In truth, it is not a physical entity at all. Rather it is a manifestation of a spiritual idea, the purpose of which is to enhance our spiritual evolution. In other words, at this stage of our development we needed a body to be able to move from place to place and have diverse experiences. That is one of the things that defines life on the earthly plane: all living creatures on this plane have a manifested body. But whether it is a fish or a tree or a man body, in no way does the body of the creature comprise its essential identity. Rather it is always merely an idea or appearance, manifested for the purpose of function ability and growth. Never was the body of a creature intended to be an independent physical entity to become attached to and identified with. For us humans, this has been a perversion of the Adam mind—one of the key erroneous beliefs that has kept us stuck.

Thus we find that the human body is actually spiritual in composition. That is why it can be said that it was created in the perfection of being. Spirit is never and indeed cannot be imperfect. In the same way that God is perfect, all spiritual creations of God are also perfect. As we come to understand this, we realize that only a digression in spiritual consciousness can affect the body with seeming imperfection. Not only this, but we also realize that the condition of the body is strictly a matter of spiritual governance. This was what Jesus meant, when he taught: "The eye is the lamp of the body. If your eyes are good, your whole body will be full of light. But if your eyes are bad, your whole body will be full of darkness. If then the light within you is darkness, how great is that darkness." (Matthew 6:22,23). Was Jesus concerned with our physical eyesight in this passage? No, of course not. He was talking about a spiritual dynamic, in which either light or darkness emanates from consciousness and acts upon our body. Moreover, he warns us that if we allow ourselves to be governed by spiritual darkness—i.e. Adamic consciousness—we are in for big trouble. This then is the spiritual principle behind healing: the consciousness that acts upon our body for good is the consciousness of light or God union, while the consciousness that acts upon our body for evil is the consciousness of darkness or the Adam mind; therefore the key to healing is to change our consciousness to light (make our eye single), which will in turn act for good upon our body.

Disease then is really a spiritual digression caused by the unconscious governance of the Adam mind over our inner world. The devastation behind our second door is the devastation of Adamic consciousness, just as it is behind all our doors, manifesting in this case as bodily dysfunction. As long as the Adam mind is holding sway and acting upon our inner world, all our doors will present a picture of devastation. Why? Because the Adam mind *is* spiritual darkness, and when we are unconscious of that fact, how great is that darkness!

Behind our second door the practical outworking of this debilitating spiritual dynamic can be expressed in different ways. One of these is the oppressive treatment of the body by the prodigal mind. The attitude of the prodigal toward his or her body is generally one of exploitation. This is because the prodigal is caught up in a perceived Darwinian struggle to survive, and it uses the body as one of its foremost aids in pursuing this agenda. Under this regimen the body is literally forced to exert strength far beyond its means and move at an unnatural rhythm and pace. It is placed under stresses and strains it was never created to bear. Minimally it must earn the prodigal's livelihood by the sweat of its brow. The prodigal mind rarely shows concern for the body that does its bidding. Rather it treats it as a kind of slave.

Also the Adam mind is extremely indiscriminate when it comes to indulging in negative emotions such as fear, hatred, and resentment. It often panders to these without restraint, justifying their overpowering effect by pointing to adverse circumstances as their instigator and reasonable motive for perpetuation. But these emotions act like poison in our bodies. The more we give them free rein, the more the organic systems of the body are thrown into disarray.

The Adam mind would have us believe that the human body is immune to this kind of irresponsible mental-emotional treatment. It paints the picture that the body can take such doses of abuse without any harm being done. And maybe for a time this proves true. But eventually our mental ill treatment of the body catches up to us in the form of bodily dysfunction and disease.

Is the human body invincible? Obviously not. In fact, the truth of the matter is that it is far more vulnerable than we like to believe. Its complex organic systems interact according to a delicately balanced creative mandate. Thus it does not take much for this balance to be upended. Certainly the kind of abuse imposed by the desperate prodigal agenda is enough to cause major problems. Also the toxic chemical reaction caused by heavy negative emotionalism is a sure recipe for disaster.

When we consider the full impact of this devastation being played out in the inner body register of each individual in our world, we understand that not only are disease and bodily dysfunction rampant in our midst; they are epidemic. This gross impediment to individual wholeness and well-being has spilled over into the collective arena, so that society at large has become largely obsessed with the issue of health care and in so doing has demanded action on the part of our doctors and scientists. These have answered the call and through diligence and hard work have developed medical science to the point that it can now treat and cure many of the ailments of modern man. This it has accomplished by learning to isolate each of the body's organic systems and use medicines to either increase or diminish a particular organ's function ability, thereby restoring balance to the entire organism. In this way doctors have become the saviors of many a modern world citizen. There is only one problem. Since the body is acted upon primarily by consciousness, it is not uncommon for the diseases and imbalances recently corrected to soon reappear. The particular organ affected may change, but the brand of devastation bears a strong resemblance to that which the doctors have cured.

Thus there is in actuality only one solution for the plague of disease and bodily dysfunction: saying *no* to Adamic consciousness and *yes* to the new consciousness of God union and the realization of God's presence within us. This is how we put an end once and for all to the negative effect of the Adam mind acting upon our body and shift that effect to the benign healing power of God's active presence. Once we have effectually brought this shift to pass, our body is freed from the influence of the Adam mind and brought under the governance of divine creative law.

What then ensues is a two-fold transformation in our bodily condition. The first effect of this transformation is that of healing and restoring the body to its natural created mandate. Many of us who have been under the governance of the Adam mind have never known freedom from bodily dysfunction. Throughout our lifetime our body has operated primarily in response to our own strength and will. We have therefore never experienced the relaxed, natural mode of functioning for which our body was created. But when we say *yes* to the new consciousness, immediately the divine power begins to act upon our body and bring about the transformation from the patched-up state of health we had forged in our own prodigal strength to the state of health that is reflective of God's perfect creative principle. This is the mystery of healing. In truth, it is not a miracle; it is a restoration to our created estate.

The second effect builds on our healing-restorative experience by establishing us permanently in that state. Perfect bodily health is not difficult to maintain once we have opened ourselves up to God's healing consciousness and learned to live by the divine laws of the body's creative principle. The care and habits that lead to optimal function ability are not beyond the understanding of the average person. They are not the exclusive domains of scientists. Rather much of health care is a matter of common sense and can be learned and implemented quite fluidly once we have been set free from the destructive tyranny of the Adam mind. Many a chronic ailment brought on through years of weakness and oppression can be quickly dissolved by such regimens as improved diet, getting better rest, and paying heed to habitual abusive tendencies. Likewise, the gradual weaning off of negative emotionalism works wonders. In any case, when it comes to maintaining the wonderful effects of a recently healed body, we will not lack for incentive. For, having tasted of life free from bodily pain, dysfunction, and disease at last, we will never want to go back to our former compromised condition.

The Supply Register

Our third door is the door of supply, behind which we deal with issues of livelihood and provision. As with our first two doors, when we open the door of the supply register we behold two distinct possibilities and potentialities, only here as they pertain to supply. One potentiality is the harmonious alignment with the flow of supply we were created to enjoy—that which the Bible calls *living by grace.* The other is the devastation of being out of harmony with God's grace and given over to the pursuit of supply in our own natural human strength and ingenuity—that which the Bible calls *the curse of Adam* or having to earn our bread by the sweat of our brow (Genesis 3:19). Along with the existence of these two potential approaches we also learn of their associated fruits or demonstrations. We see that to live by grace is to never have to worry or even take thought for our supply needs, while to live under the Adam curse is to perpetually suffer the effects of lack and limitation to one degree or another. Finally we learn that these two divergent demonstrations are directly attributable to our state of spiritual consciousness.

The need for supply is an inescapable aspect of human life. Every single person born into our world must have at least the basics of supply in order to survive. And sometimes, when supply is utterly lacking for one reason or another, the results can be tragic. But as with our second door, what most people do not realize is that supply is actually a spiritual reality. In our culture people tend to think that it is only a pragmatic matter of dollars and cents. They see supply as the acquisition, getting, and accumulating of wealth or material goods, whereas, in truth, the quality of our supply is not about how much we possess; it is about which state of spiritual consciousness is holding sway in our inner world.

There is a supply that belongs to us as a species, according to our created mandate. This is true because all creatures in our universe were created with the idea of their supply accompanying their appearance. No creature that was made—and this implies a mind-boggling array of diversity—entered our world without its supply already arranged and seen to. What this means is that for most creatures getting supply is not a strain or an effort. It requires no cleverness or strength. It is simply a natural dynamic that happens fluidly and harmoniously. Man also, as a created being, entered this world with his supply already seen to. All he had to do to enjoy the fruits of this provision was to stay consciously connected to and aligned with the source that provided it. But after man adopted the consciousness of Adam—that is, of willful prodigality—he saw himself as separate and cut off from the created source. That was when man's supply troubles began.

Instead of relaxing and trusting that his needs would be met according to God's omniscient creative mandate, the Adam man had to find his own way to be supplied. And it is this independent initiative concerning supply that has been one of the foremost causes of suffering in the human ranks. Indeed it has turned out to be a curse, just as was prophesized in the Parable of the Garden.

Adamic consciousness is an aberration from our created mandate across the board. But nowhere is this more glaringly evident than here behind our third door. Supply never needed to be an issue for us. Instead it has become a terrible plague in our midst and resulted in great societal inequality and suffering.

The plague associated with modern man's supply does not involve amounts or degrees of sufficiency. Rather it is reflective of the *quality* of our supply. In other words, in terms of actual abundance, a wealthy man in our society probably has more than he would have had, had he received his supply from God's grace. This is because, when God originally created and supplied us the emphasis was not on *how much*; it was on simply *having a sufficiency that met our need and enabled us to live without having to be anxious or take thought*. The fact that we would not have to take thought would be the indication of the perfect outworking of this aspect of human life. It is a little like wearing an outfit of clothes that fits so perfectly, we forget that we have it on. This is the difference between the supply that comes to us as a result of Adamic consciousness and that which comes to us when we are aligned harmoniously with the source through grace. It is not how much; it is how problem-free it feels.

The devastation of Adamic consciousness that we find behind our third door is a stigmatic, unshakable sense of lack and limitation. In extreme cases it manifests as abject poverty and can make life insufferable. But for most of us modern Westerners it is not abject poverty that colors our experience; it is a vague, frustrating sense that what we have in the way of supply is not enough; it is too limiting, confining, and finite. In other words, we have supply, but we are never happy with the quality of that supply.

Had we stayed connected to God and aligned with the supply that accompanied our creation, this matter of quality would never have been an issue. That perfect supply carries no stigma of lack and limitation. But we did not stay true to our created mandate. Rather we ventured into the realm of Adamic consciousness. This venturing not only made it difficult to live by grace; it made it virtually impossible. This is because the prodigal Adam mind has cut itself off from the source. Through its insistent agenda of independent Darwinian manifest destiny it has come to see itself as separate from God. Therefore God's supply must remain off limits to it.

And yet, obviously we still needed supply. So there developed a different approach for our species. Instead of receiving our supply effortlessly from the storehouse of God, we learned to earn it by the sweat of our brow. Instead of taking no thought, we learned to plot and scheme, connive and manipulate. Instead of our supply coming to us as a natural flow of universal law, we learned to make it happen proactively—to get, to acquire, and to hoard. But in doing all this, we discovered something we had not reckoned on. We discovered that the supply we caused to come to us proactively turned out to be of a different quality than the supply that comes from the source: God.

How can two kinds of supply differ in quality and manifestation? Would not the supply be the same, regardless of which methods were used to attain it? The answer is *no*. The supply itself is different.

The supply that comes from God, the source, is self-renewing and replenishing. Like the manna that fell in the wilderness and supplied the nutritional needs of the Israelites for forty years, without them sowing, reaping, or harvesting during that entire period, it is new every morning. And most distinctly, it is of infinite quality—that is to say, it comes to us free of any trace or semblance of lack and limitation. Contrastingly, the supply that has become associated with prodigality and human striving is non-renewing and finite. It is static and elusive. The moment we get it, it begins to escape our grasp and dwindle. This requires that we exert enormous amounts of energy, not only to get supply, but also to keep it and protect it.

We have already seen how the true supply comes to us from the source fluidly and effortlessly, when we align ourselves harmoniously with the divine law of grace. But how does the prodigal approach work?

First, let us remember that at the present time we are a society of prodigals—seven billion strong. Thus it is that the prodigal approach to getting supply has become the norm, while the approach of living by grace has become the aberration. This means that the prodigal approach is totally accepted in human society, even when it crosses over into unavoidable gray areas of immorality and scamming. The sad fact is that in most cases one who has honed the prodigal approach to a perfected science so that they have become wealthy is not merely accepted; he or she is greatly admired and envied.

Basically, the prodigal approach has as its goal and impetus the acquisition of already existing supply. In other words, though the prodigal is cut off from God's perfect renewable supply, he discovers that supply already exists in the world of men in pockets of affluence, whether those pockets belong to individuals, companies, or governments. The task before him then becomes how to coax some of this existing supply from the hands of these human sources and into his own possession. This coaxing activity has become so acceptable and taken for granted in our society that it is now one of the true underpinnings cementing our present societal order. This can be seen by the fact that even career endeavors and employment fall under this approach. When we dissect the true chemistry behind the common pursuit of employment what we find is an individual in need of supply approaching an individual or company that has an abundance of existing supply and entering in to a contractual agreement with them to channel some of that excess toward them in exchange for services or labors rendered. Then in accordance with this agreement, the employed individual is paid a certain amount of money each week or month—an amount represented by numbers on a piece of paper we call a paycheck. But anyone that has received a paycheck for any length of time can testify that one of the true stigmas of this arrangement is the sense of lack and limitation it promotes. It is not long before those agreed-upon numbers on the paycheck begin to feel finite, stagnant, and boxed-in.

Now suppose one decides to break out of the rut of lack and limitation associated with employment and paychecks. Suppose he decides to venture out into the world of entrepreneurial enterprise. This can be a gamble of course. But let us suppose that this adventurous person succeeds in attracting larger amounts of existing supply than he had been able to earn under the contractual employment arrangement. Let us even suppose that this man becomes wealthy. Will he at last escape the devastation of lack and limitation? Unfortunately, he will not. Rather to his great consternation, he will find that his supply, though more expansive, is still finite, static, and limiting. Why is this? Because that is the nature of existing supply, and it does not matter whether one has a lot or a little.

It is therefore nothing more than a grand deception that our culture paints the picture of the acquisition of wealth being a sure road to happiness. Not only are we taught that wealth is the answer to supply problems, but we are also encouraged to continue on that same course, should our problems persist. In other words, if after accruing a half million dollars, we still feel the devastation of lack and limitation, the solution is to get a million. Always the accrued amount that will finally end the curse lay just in front of us. But this is simply not true, as many have learned by experience. As long as we are dealing with existing supply, the amount we accrue will not alleviate our distress. Lack and limitation will continue to dog us and make us miserable.

Only through a change of consciousness can we reverse the devastation of lack and limitation, because only through changing our consciousness to the awareness of God's presence and activity in our inner world will we be able to realign with the source and become the recipients of God's grace. Only by saying *no* to the prodigal Adam mind can we reverse the curse of earning our bread by the sweat of our brow.

According to our species' created mandate there is already in place a designated flow of supply for us to align with and receive effortlessly and without taking thought. This supply differs from the existing supply we see in the various affluent pockets of human society. It is neither finite nor limiting. It is new every morning and self-replenishing. It is completely void of the stigma of lack and limitation.

The Soul Register

Our fourth door is unique by virtue of its transcendent quality. It deals with the status and condition of our eternal soul. Therefore it is really more than an aspect of our inner workings; it is essentially their sum total.

Everybody has an eternal soul, and it is this quality of universal timeless continuance that lends our soul its transcendent nature. Up until now our concerns, while spiritual and inward, have been largely temporal and spatial. We have been reversing devastations that have to do with this present lifetime—our health, our supply, and even our mortality. Now what we find as we enter our fourth door is that it is the fractured condition of our eternal soul that is the root cause of all the other devastations. Correspondingly, it is the healing of our soul sickness that brings everything else about our being into harmonious alignment with God.

Not surprisingly then, gaining the degree of spiritual consciousness that can set our soul condition right is no easy task. For one thing, the level of unconsciousness and ignorance surrounding soul realities in modern Western culture is appalling. Few of us are aware of or in touch with this essential part of us. From birth we are taught to identify ourselves with our body and our ego—both of which are temporal realities. Therefore most of us do not know our eternal selves at all. We live this entire life as if in a dream of temporal thoughts, feelings, sensations, and concerns. Like a horse with blinders on, we completely miss the eternal quality of human existence.

As we embark upon the journey of spiritual consciousness development, however, we soon learn what we have been missing. We come to realize that though we have been ignoring our soul, it has not been ignoring us. In countless ways our soul has been trying to get us to wake up and pay attention. In fact, it is not overstating the matter to say that in most people their soul is literally screaming to them to come home.

Yes, being soul sick is like being absent from ourselves. We are a race that is self-estranged and alienated. For most of us this condition begins at birth. Somehow the decision was made (either by us or for us) that we must leave our soul register, shut the door behind us, and never go back, not even for a visit. Perhaps this was an instinctual reaction on our part. It is as if we took one look at the unclean condition of our soul and immediately made the judgment that the situation was hopeless. Also we saw others around us in the same boat. In fact, the entire emphasis in our culture is on escaping the soul. Thus we understood that there is no human solution to this problem, other than to run from it. Science has no answers; accumulating wealth is of no avail. Only avoidance seems to work for us, and in terms of justification, it certainly helps that our culture teaches that not only is this the best way; it is also perfectly harmless. In other words, not only are we encouraged to flee from our soul register, but we also are impressed upon that such an approach is actually normal and nothing to be concerned about.

Unfortunately, the only way we can be unconcerned about this is to live life as if under a shroud of delusion. We are a broken, fractured people. At the very source of our being is a major weakness and foundational flaw. In cutting ourselves off and becoming estranged from our eternal soul we have missed the entire point of being alive. We have virtually guaranteed that this life will be lived only for temporal purposes and rewards, and as everyone knows, all such rewards must be utterly relinquished when we die.

What then is this devastation behind our fourth door that causes even the strongest among men to run and view escape as a reasonable and sane choice? It is the unclean effect of the Adam mind upon the human soul; it is what the Bible calls sin. This is a very volatile word, mostly due to our cultural conditioning. But volatility in no way means that we have understood it rightly. Our religions assert that sin is a kind of compilation of our moral lapses and bad deeds. But spiritual consciousness sees the matter a little differently. It asserts that sin is nothing more than a climate of uncleanness in our soul register—a climate so unpleasant and ugly that it makes it literally impossible for us to embrace ourselves. True, this climate has been enhanced and perpetuated through our moral lapses and misdeeds, but once it is established it makes little difference if we add a lapse here or a misdeed there. Once the climate of uncleanness becomes unclean, it stays that way. This is because sin is the *effect* of Adamic consciousness.

This was what Jesus meant when he taught about knowing a tree by its fruit: "Do people pick grapes from thorn bushes, or figs from thistles? Likewise every good tree bears good fruit, but a bad tree bears bad fruit." (Matthew 7:16,17). The *tree* Jesus spoke of is our state of consciousness. In this analogy a bad tree—i.e. Adamic consciousness—bears bad fruit—i.e. sin and leads to the dis integration of our soul. On the other hand, a good tree—i.e. the new consciousness—bears good fruit and results in reintegration.

Sin then is an unclean condition of soul brought about through our adherence to Adamic consciousness. It renders the climate of our soul register so foul that our primary instinct is to flee. To this end we are encouraged and supported by the cultural mandate of this present world, which not only justifies escape in this case, but even ennobles it.

The awakening of individual consciousness then is very much related to the sin question. This is because only a change in consciousness can bring about the healing and reintegration of our fractured soul. For this reason Jesus came and dwelt among us as the embodiment of God's redemptive power. He knew that unless and until we dealt with the sin question, our soul register would remain a no-man's-land. He also knew that the way to vanquish the effects of sin forever was through a change in consciousness that released the activity of God into our inner world.

In the new consciousness we reverse the devastations of unconsciousness and the Adam mind in all their manifestations in our inner world, including the plague of sin in our soul register. By saying *yes* to the presence and activity of God's Spirit within us, we bring God's redemptive principle to bear upon our hopeless soul condition. Then through this divine power our soul register is cleansed, renewed, and made habitable again. In fact, after God has had Its way with our soul register, it becomes such a lovely and inviting place that we are not only willing to return; we literally are chomping at the bit. For, the return to our soul register after being absent for an entire lifetime is truly something to rejoice about. It is more than a temporal sensation of healing; it is the sensation of having finally come home, both to God and ourselves.

Chapter Seven

Redemption and Reintegration

The goal of all spiritual undertaking (and this could well be pursued over many lifetimes) is reintegration with our own individual soul. For, it is impossible to aspire to God union until we have become unified within ourselves. A fractured soul condition must necessarily result in a temporal misdirected life view. True, we can exist as human beings for seventy or eighty years, but when we die we will have accomplished nothing of any spiritual-eternal worth. We will have done nothing more than waste a precious opportunity—that as represented by human birth.

It is our spiritual consciousness that determines our soul condition. The experience of being born as a human being into this present world order is one of embracing Adamic consciousness, at least initially. This means that every one of us, with very few exceptions, will suffer the estrangement from our own soul that leads to dis integration. In a world dominated by Adamic consciousness this is normal and natural. Modern human culture supports and facilitates soul dis integration. It welcomes us into the fold of the self-estranged and presents us with a very elaborate alternative life view. It downplays the significance and importance of soul reintegration, until we finally come to accept the fact that we must live this life locked out of our own soul register and make the best of it.

There are two main reasons that we seek to escape our soul register: one is that it is emotionally painful to stay, and the other is that we know of no other solution than to leave. Emotionally, our guilt and fear overwhelm us. We know that something is not right when we feel alienated from our own soul and we sense that this is a matter of weighty spiritual repercussion, but our fruitless attempts at correction frustrate us and wear us out. We may be amenable to the idea of soul reintegration, but eventually our emotional state and wrong beliefs win out. When this happens, we throw in our lot with the rest of humanity and join the ranks of the dis integrated. After that we gain some distance from our soul issues and tend to take things less to heart. Just as the world culture teaches, we find that soul reintegration is not crucial to our survival. We can still live a decent, prosperous, and even happy life without it. We can carve out our own little niche in this world order and find a degree of fulfillment therein. We can focus our energies on career aspirations and uplifting social configurations. In short, we can distract and delude ourselves successfully and affirmatively right up until the day we die.

What we fail to realize is that somewhere—in some deep part of our being—our dis integration has hurt us. It has robbed us of spiritual life and rendered God's joy and goodness off limits to us. And perhaps worst of all, it has turned human life into a pointless exercise in temporal futility.

All of this is the result of spiritual consciousness; it is the Adam mind having its way with us on account of our own ignorance and unconsciousness. In other words, it does not have to be this way for us. True, it is tough when we are born into a world that operates twenty-four-seven under the dream-like influence of the Adam mind. But at any given time we can awaken from that dream and change our state of consciousness—from Adamic to the new consciousness of God realization that leads to soul reintegration.

This is the beauty of spiritual consciousness. It is a realm of endless potentialities. When the light of truth dawns within us, it always brings about the effects of abundance and goodness that Jesus referred to as *eternal life*. But before this can happen for us, we have to be able to honestly assess our condition. We need to understand our own role in the development of spiritual consciousness and not shirk that responsibility. And we must have faith in God—minimally that God exists as impersonal omnipresent Spirit and can be a source of inspiration and strength to us in our quest.

When we gain the revelation that it is Adamic consciousness that has created the unbearable conditions in our soul, we have taken a huge step in the right direction. When we can stand our ground long enough to say, "Though this looks hopeless, I believe that with God all things are possible," we have begun the process of reintegration. For, instead of running and escaping, we are showing that we value spiritual realities—specifically, the concept of being able to dwell within our own soul in peace. We are saying *yes* to the new consciousness to act as a power in our inner world and set things right.

The Redemptive Principle as an Activity of God

We would be deceiving ourselves, however, to think that this is an undertaking we can accomplish without God. When we stand and honestly behold the blighted condition of our soul, we must acknowledge that we, in and of ourselves, are powerless to amend it. What can a man do about sin? No, as the New Testament says, "Who can forgive sin but God alone?" (Luke 5:21).

The new consciousness is not the consciousness of man's inherent spiritual capabilities; it is the consciousness of God's presence felt within and God's activity being set in motion through our conscious awareness. There is a huge distinction here. A man cannot deal with the mess of an unclean sin-sick soul, but he can, through developing his spiritual consciousness, learn how to release God's active presence and thereby receive the divine power that can and will make amends.

God's activity has a specific demonstration for the reversal of all of the inner devastations brought about through our embracing of Adamic consciousness. Behind our first door we watched as

God responded to the plague of death by sending in streams of living water—the water of eternal-resurrection life. Behind our second door we saw disease and bodily dysfunction give way to God's healing restorative principle of grace and the perfection of being. Behind our third door we were able to relinquish our wrongful approach to getting supply and by grace become realigned with the true supply we were created to enjoy—supply void of the stigma of lack and limitation. Now here at our fourth door—our soul register—we find ourselves acknowledging that we need God's help more than ever.

Behind the first three doors we could conceive of at least quasi-solutions to the devastations confronting us. In the absence of eternal life we could learn to be satisfied with a typical lifespan of seventy or eighty years and try to get as much out of those years as possible. In the face of disease and recurring bodily dysfunction we could put our trust in medical science and get regularly patched up sufficiently enough to go on. And whenever feeling constrained and oppressed by the stigma of lack and limitation inherent in the approach of coaxing existing supply, we could determine to work harder and try to get more. But here at our fourth door we feel completely helpless and utterly bereft of solutions.

All the sin and uncleanness of a lifetime have accumulated here in our soul register, with our only recourse being to try to push it into a pile in the corner of our psyche, out of sight and out of mind. But eventually that pile grows to the point of being unmanageable. Here the karmic wheel churns away loudly and incessantly, causing a carry over of sin and uncleanness from our past into our present, so that even when we are not sinning in the moment our karma muddies our present consciousness of soul. Here we also must face our weakness and sense of neediness. Our sin-sick soul condition has rendered us unsure of ourselves and vulnerable to temptation. We feel that we need some kind of help or support, if we are to go on. But this only causes us to open the door to yet greater soul defilement. Woe to us! As the leper in Jesus' day was taught to call out, "Unclean, unclean," whenever he ventured among uninfected people, so we too can only cry out, "Unclean, unclean." Indeed to be unclean of soul is a far worse condition than to be unclean in body.

The good news is that there is a divine antidote to sin and soul uncleanness: the redemptive principle of God. This principle is neither new nor sovereignly instigated. It is not given or withheld. It has always been there and always will be there. It is scientifically established as an activity of God. Thus just as we found a specific demonstration of God's activity and power operating behind each of our first three doors, we now discover this wonderful truth: *the demonstration of God's activity operating behind our fourth door or soul register is the unconditional, all-inclusive principle of redemptive forgiveness.* Like the other activities of God operating in our inner world, this wondrous redemptive principle is unleashed through the activity of our own spiritual consciousness. It is our conscious *yes* to the presence and activity of God that reverses the devastations that the Adam mind has wrought in our soul.

This redemptive principle as an activity of God in our soul register is not to be confused with the orthodox religious doctrine spoken of in the New Testament. It is true that the power of redemption can come to us through faith in the cross of the Messiah Jesus. But it is equally true that God's redemptive principle was already operational in the world just awaiting our consciousness development in order to be activated. What Jesus' sacrificial death was meant to accomplish was to shine a light of awareness on this already existing divine institution, so that our spiritual consciousness could develop to where we could understand the divine dynamic and learn to set it in motion.

Receiving the revelation of God's redemptive principle can come to us through an abiding faith in Jesus, but the actual mechanics of setting that principle in motion in such a way that it cleanses and renews our soul register has little to do with Jesus. Rather it has to do with our own spiritual consciousness development. If there is any fault to be attributed to the orthodox teaching of the doctrine of redemption, it involves the portrayal of God as being a separate and aloof super being, who has condescended to grant us forgiveness of sin through Jesus' atoning sacrifice as an act of mercy, which at times He regrets having done. What is missing is the right knowledge of God and the scientific impersonal quality of all of God's activities, including redemption. It is the understanding that redemption is offered to us, not out of some sovereign divine impulse, but rather because it is a part of God's eternal nature.

There is also a false sense in Christendom that redemption is personal and must be earned. From Church pulpits we can rightly ascertain that we need God's forgiveness for sin and that forgiveness is a healing balm for our soul, but we fail to hear the message that God's forgiveness is unconditional and impersonal. Somehow this one aspect of false teaching undermines the power of the redemptive principle. We want to believe that our sins are forgiven, but how can we be sure when it is a personal matter with God? What if God should change His mind? What if we were to commit the unpardonable sin? Any number of variables could conceivably enter into the picture to render us doubtful.

This is not to say, however, that the Church teaching is entirely without merit. For one thing, it is through believing in Jesus as the Lamb of God that takes away the sin of the world that our consciousness initially opens to the truth about our own sin-sick soul condition and the possibility of a redemptive response from heaven. This is what Jesus' messianic commission was really all about—the opening of our spiritual consciousness to truth and new possibilities. Nevertheless, as we grow spiritually we come to realize that there is no power in adhering to a doctrine or simply claiming its benefits. The power comes as we develop our consciousness through recognizing the truth about our inner condition as wrought by the devastations of the Adam mind and then scientifically ascertaining God's true nature. We must *experience* redemption as an inviolable truth about God—one that is in no way personal or conditional. Only then can the redemptive principle become the corrective power in our soul register that it was meant to be.

The redemptive principle unleashed through our conscious *yes* is an activity of God—a part of God's nature—that acts like divine law. It is as certain as the sun coming up in the morning and lighting up the daytime sky. It has been in operation since before Abraham was—that is, since creation. Jesus did not invent it. All he did was to bring it to the forefront of our conscious awareness, so that we could learn the truth and integrate that truth into our spiritual consciousness.

The Outworking of Redemption

Let us suppose then that we are ready in terms of our spiritual consciousness development to say *yes* to the presence and activity of God, manifesting as the redemptive principle in our soul register. What happens next?

Remember that we once considered the devastation brought upon our soul register by the Adam mind to be so daunting and ugly that all we could do was to leave, shut the door behind us, and escape into the arms of a soulless, dis integrated world. So the first thing we need to do is to muster the courage to open that door again and face our fears.

Sure enough, our former actions were not totally unreasonable. The devastation we behold when we reopen this door strikes us as even more terrible than we remember it being. We see sin and guilt piled far and high. This pile is so rancid that it is crawling with worms and emits a stench. It makes our stomach turn and our senses reel. Then we become aware of a loud grinding noise. It is the karmic wheel churning, churning, churning, and bringing a steady flow of past sin and uncleanness into our present moment. This wheel has been in operation throughout our entire lifetime. It consistently adds sin to the pile, even when that sin has no basis in the present moment. It is old sin—sin from past lives.

Walking over a little ways, we see an open door, which we ourselves had once opened prior to making our escape. Suddenly we notice for the first time—another stream of uncleanness and defilement flowing in through this open door. Jogging our memory, it all comes back to us. This was the door to friendship with the world. Once long ago we had opened it, looking for help and support in our soul plight. We had felt so desperate, looking for help anywhere we could. We had heard that there was help to be found in the world among our fellowman. And indeed we had found helpful attitudes, supportive glances, and even some genuine kindness, but when push came to shove nobody gave us what we needed. Thus we came to acknowledge the wisdom in the Bible, when it compares turning to Egypt (a symbol of this world) for help to leaning on a broken staff. Just when you least expect it, the staff breaks under your weight, and your condition is worse than it was in the beginning. Yes, the world pretended to be helpful, but it only amounted to clouds without rain. How could it be otherwise in a world of seven billion prodigals, each one fighting for his or her piece of the pie? Every offer of help, when unmasked, was exposed as a scheme of self-serving and prodigal juxtapositioning. The people at the bank, who wanted to "help" by loaning money, were only doing it for their own monetary gain. The people at the church sponsored soup kitchen were only feeding the poor in order to feel good about themselves, etc., etc., etc. Once long ago we had naively sought friendship with the world, only to become disillusioned and flee from our soul register. But why had we forgotten to close that door? Obviously, that had been a serious oversight. For, ever since then an unclean flow had been entering our inner world through it—the flow of world mesmerism. What is world mesmerism? It is the spirit of the dominant Darwinian prodigal mindset expressed as an indisputable reality view. And because it is a lying spirit, it is unclean. Thus its flow is just one more source of defilement in our already burdened soul register.

As if the devastations of sin, guilt, karma, and world mesmerism had not been enough to make us flee, we suddenly remember one other source of uncleanness that was so ensnaring it bordered on a form of enslavement. Again, this was something we brought upon ourselves through ignorance, weakness, and neediness. It involved our relationships with our fellow human beings.

In the parable of the prodigal son one of the truly defining aspects of his prodigal experience is described in this short sentence: "He began to be in need." (Luke 15:14). When we walk away from our soul register, we become prodigals. And when we become prodigals, we inevitably begin to be in need. It is this same sense of neediness that caused us to succumb to the temptation of friendship with the world and open the door to the defiling flow of world mesmerism. But where we really got in trouble was when, out of our need, we opened our hearts to the hope that being emotionally involved with others would meet that need and give meaning and purpose to our lives. This is as big of a deception as friendship with the world, but it is more difficult to detect and far more difficult to extricate ourselves from, once we have seen the truth.

The idea that other people can satisfy our neediness and fulfill us goes back to our childhood socio-psychological conditioning. As we are growing up we are taught that being involved with people is one of the keys to living a happy, full life. We are taught that it is normal to need people, depend on people, use people, and take everything that people have to offer us. Thus we are encouraged to seek out such relationships and are confident that what we are seeking will come to pass.

The most binding form of human involvement is marriage. Since we have been conditioned to pursue this as the ultimate fulfillment in this lifetime, it is pretty much a given that most people will try it at least once, and many end up trying it several times with different partners. Rarely, however, even among those who have had jaded experiences in this arena, is it seen for what it truly is: a source of spiritual uncleanness that we willingly invite into our soul register.

It is not our marriage partners or other family members that are unclean; it is the dynamic of emotional entanglement. Such a dynamic would not even exist if everyone were integrated, whole, and fully responsible. But remember, we are a society of prodigals—that is, of dis integrated, fractured people. We are all prodigals—seven billion strong. As such, we are all fending for ourselves and trying desperately to make our own way. Thus emotional entanglement is a given in almost all relationships, since it is through emotional manipulation that we have learned to get what we want and need.

Many, many people are involved in relationships, whether of the family or friendship variety, that are unclean on account of the dynamic of emotional manipulation. This dynamic acts like cords of entanglement that wrap around us and choke the very life out of us. It is therefore a form of soul uncleanness that is both cruel and oppressive.

So as we reopen the door to our soul register we will in all likelihood find that in addition to the uncleanness caused by sin, guilt, karma, and world mesmerism we are also involved in at least one and possibly several relationships that are emotionally entangling. This then completes the picture of our soul register's unclean condition. No wonder we judged the situation as hopeless and bailed.

But now we are back with a newly developed spiritual consciousness—a consciousness that empowers us to unleash God's redemptive principle as an activity in our inner world. Through the *yes* of our own spiritual consciousness, we now have the hope that our soul is no longer a lost cause. And yet, the situation looks even more daunting than it did when we left. It appears to have worsened during the years of our absence and neglect. A part of us doubts if even God is able to clean up such a mess.

Thankfully, however, God is up to the task. The redemptive principle goes right to work, forgiving our sin and removing our guilt. Why is God doing this for us, we might wonder? Then we remember the great truth about God's scientific impersonal universal nature. God is not doing it for us personally. God is simply doing what God does—that is, impersonally bringing redemption to another sin-sick human soul.

And so we watch in amazement as our soul register is cleansed, purified, and made new. Our sins are forgiven and forgotten; our guilt is removed as far as the east is from the west, and the karmic wheel within us is not just given a break, but is completely and permanently shut down. The cogs in its machinery grind to a halt, never to start up again. The flow of karma from our past lives ceases, and simultaneously we are renewed in the present. We also take note of the deep quietude that results from this development. We had never before realized how loud the karmic wheel was when it was in full swing and how immensely that noise pollution had added to our soul's discomfiture.

Then even as we are watching this great miracle take place and processing its full implications, we become aware of a new strength and resolve growing within us. We look over and see the door of world mesmerism flapping in the breeze and we determine to go over and shut it on our own volition. Lastly, we discern the emotionally entangling quality of some of our relationships, and a strong desire takes hold of us to be freed from these cords of bondage. So one by one we address these dishonest situations and bring them into the light of truth.

Before we know it, our lives are wonderfully clean and problem-free. As with our other three doors, the activity of God released by our own spiritual consciousness in the form of redemption has reversed the devastation of soul dis integration, and it has done so thoroughly and decisively. In great joy we become aware of the still small voice within saying these words to us: "There, now you are clean again; go and sin no more."

Reintegration

"Blessed are those who wash their robes, that they may have the right to the tree of life and may go through the gates into the city." (Revelation 22:14).

There is no better way to describe the feelings associated with soul reintegration than as the ultimate homecoming. The city referred to in the scripture above is our own soul—the soul from which we have been banished for the better part of our lives.

There is no great mystery to this soul restoration or to the power of God's redemptive principle. The mystery is how and why we became so thoroughly estranged from our own Self in the first place. Dis integration occurred as a result of our own decision to abandon our soul realm and shut the door behind us. Fracturing and devastation followed as surely as night follows day. But what was the impetus behind our decision? When did we make it, and what was the reason for it? These are the true mysteries of life. What God has created is consistent and true, but all that man has done as an expression of his desire for soul expulsion remains muddy and contradictory.

It is God that now washes our robes and sanctifies our soul register, thereby making it into a habitable realm of delight instead of a place of torment and shame. As we behold the wonder of God's redemptive power, we then negotiate the return. Our experience is a little like having a real estate agent come to us in our old neighborhood—a neighborhood filled with violence and crime—and take us to show us a new home in a new neighborhood—a wonderful neighborhood where there is peace, quiet, and dignity. The Spirit of God is that agent. "Do you want to move in?" It asks us, showing us around a soul register that is now so transformed and lovely we never would have believed that it was ours. Our response is swift and unwavering. "Yes, yes!" we cry out. And so it is done.

This is the true return to the Father's house. It is the return to our right mind. This one act of consciousness makes everything right. It makes everything fall into place. Having access to the tree of life, we now gain the revelation that our life is indeed indestructible—that nothing can ever harm us again. Suddenly we see everything clearly—no longer as if through a glass darkly but rather face to face. We are now able to know God aright and worship in Spirit and truth. At last, God union can become a reality.

With reintegration also comes the revelation that we are now no longer divided, fractured, weak, or enslaved. We are now complete and whole, lacking for no good thing. We are no longer needy or compromised. And not only is union with God now possible, but our fellowship is shown to be unbroken and indissoluble.

It is human nature that when we find a home that meets our need perfectly and in every way, we lose all desire to go or be anywhere else. Therefore our days of flight and searching come to an end. We feel no attraction whatsoever to the world of men and have no difficulty discerning its deceptive spirit. Moreover, we have no need for emotionally entangling human relationships and no hesitation about steering clear of them. Even our lifelong search for God has been laid to rest, since we now see that God is and always has been right here with us in our own soul register.

Sin is also no longer an issue in our lives. It is not that we never stray from the perfect law of righteousness in thought or deed. Rather with the ability to release God's redemptive principle through our own *yes* of conscious awareness, sin is no longer the power that it once was. It is like a toothless old lion. It can still roar, but we now know better than to be afraid of that roar. And as we learn, little by little, to look the other way, we find that sin need no longer be a source of uncleanness. God's redemptive power has removed its sting.

No longer do we need to fear what man can do to us. Coming home to our own soul register is the ultimate protective shield. It is like being ensconced in a hiding place that no one can see. It is the secret place of the Most High spoken of in the ninety-first Psalm. Thus all of our motives and energy exertions also undergo a thorough revamping. We no longer need to defend ourselves or fight our way through life. At last we find rest for our soul. It does not even matter anymore if we live or die, since our soul life is shown to be irrefutably unending. Therefore we no longer fear death.

Chapter Eight

Mystery Solved

Until we experience soul reintegration, human life will have a mysterious, foreign, and unsatisfying quality about it. For most people this quality acts as a sort of vague gnawing sense that they are missing something in their life experience—that there is something they don't know and haven't been told yet. A few among us feel so pressed by this inconsistency that they devote their lives to discovering its cause. They become philosophers or artists, or perhaps they try to find the answers through religious discipline and study. But even these sincere seekers rarely find the true answer to life's ultimate mystery.

Many people wrongly attribute life's mysterious quality to God. The irony in this approach is that not only is there no mystery to God, but God is the most sure, constant, unwavering, consistent, dependable, and trustworthy force in our universe. From where then does our mystery come? What is its source and origin? The answer is that we ourselves as a society have created this air of mystery through the promoting of a myriad of lies and justifications surrounding our irresistible inclination toward individual soul dis integration.

This inclination to abandon our soul register and willingly separate ourselves from God is what the Bible calls *sin*. The mystery is that unredeemed sin is the primary agent of uncleanness that makes us view the situation in our soul register as hopeless and therefore best dealt with through escape. And yet, it is our inclination and desire to escape in the first place that is the root of all sin. This gives rise to the proverbial question: which came first, the chicken or the egg? We seek to escape from our soul register because of the devastation caused by sin, but we originally opened the door to that devastation by desiring separation from God.

To better understand this enigma, the Bible has presented us with a powerful parabolic teaching. To testify to this parable's importance, it was placed at the very beginning of the book. Thus it is right there for us to ponder, as we begin our quest for spiritual wisdom. Unfortunately, no other biblical writing has been as widely and preposterously misinterpreted.

The first thing that the parable does is to describe the condition of the human soul, when it is fully integrated and cleansed. It gives this benign soul condition the figurative name *Eden*. In terms of time and setting, this edenic condition of soul is portrayed as being original (or created) and pre-devastation. It is also upheld as the model of a soul that has been cleansed by God's redemptive principle after the devastation of sin has had its way with it.

Eden is like a garden of delights. It is the perfection of God's being in earthly creation. It is filled with wondrous plant life, pleasing to the senses and fruitful for our provision. In it there is no time, decay, aging, or death. Rather the life therein is the eternal-resurrection life of God. There is no bodily disease or dysfunction, because all is governed in perfect spiritual harmony. And perhaps most profoundly, in Eden—that is, the fully integrated human soul—there exists unbroken fellowship with God. The soul of man walks with God in the cool shade of the garden.

Enter into this idyllic picture the devastation of sin. Suddenly the garden that was bursting with life and beauty appears blighted and withered. It becomes like our world—a world of curses and hardships. Instead of aesthetically pleasing plant life, there are bleak factories and industrial complexes puffing foul toxic smoke into the air. Instead of fruitful trees providing for our bodily needs without effort or strain, we must now earn our bread by the sweat of our brow. Instead of perfect spiritual harmony governing our body, there is a tyrannical prodigal mind forcing it into all manner of unnatural and harmful exertions. Instead of the assurance of eternal life, there is an all-consuming fear of death. And instead of unbroken fellowship with God, there is a sense of cruel binding separation.

As the parable teaches, sin begins with temptation. Thus the original sin of man is the temptation of prodigality. When this sin is acted upon and the temptation is no longer resisted, the garden of God becomes a reflection of the world of men. Being outside of the garden and fully given over to the prodigal mindset produces sin after sin, and this unredeemed sin then piles up in our soul register, causing it to become hopelessly unclean and uninhabitable.

The mystery of the parable is not the pristine condition of the sinless soul; nor is it the accursed devastation caused by sin. Rather it involves temptation. Why is there temptation in the human experience, and where does it come from? No, it does not come from a serpent crawling in the grass or a rival power to God called Satan. That is simply the parable's use of imagery and storyline. There is no rival power to God. All that God created is the perfection of being. Nevertheless, the temptation to separate ourselves from God has become an integral part of human experience, and acting upon that temptation is what has created the world of men—a world filled with mysteries, lies, and distortions.

When we decide to pack it in and desert our soul register, it is tantamount to being expelled from the garden. And so, we enter the world of men and throw in our lot with the mass of soul-escapees called the human race. In a sense it was at their behest that we took this course of action. "Look at us," they all seemed to be saying. "We left our soul registers long ago, and we're no worse for it. Its importance is overblown. Who needs it?" But life outside the garden is not very much to our liking in any case, no matter what our fellowman might say. It is unfulfilling, unhappy, and inundated with suffering and devastation. Therefore somewhere deep within us we all long for return and reintegration.

Evolving States of Consciousness

Out in the world of men most people are completely unaware that they have been expelled from the garden—that is, their own soul register. They are conditioned to believe that the life of man in this world is the only reality there is, for better or for worse. They are unaware of any temptation in their past, any decision to abandon their soul register, and any resultant willful separation from God. They acknowledge that life can be hard and at times perplexing, but that is just how it is.

This adoption of worldly realism is in actuality a state of spiritual consciousness—aptly called Adamic consciousness on account of its obvious associations with the biblical Parable of the Garden. Adamic consciousness is not the result of a judgment or curse for breaking God's command, as is usually taught. Rather it is a state of being that we find ourselves in because of spiritual consciousness evolution. In other words, based on created evolutionary law, it is where we belong. Thus we find that there is no mystery to our human predicament after all.

God created us as evolutionary creatures. Is this such a far-fetched notion? Look around at the natural world of God's creating. Many species and living creatures were created with evolutionary characteristics—from the plant that evolves from a seed into a flowering, fruit-bearing tree to the insect that begins life as a lowly worm and evolves into a soaring, colorful winged butterfly. Why should we human beings also not be evolutionary in expression? The problem is that not only do we see ourselves as static and unevolving; we also do not understand what manner of creature we are. Mistakenly, we view ourselves as individual expressions of humanity—each one unique in body and mind, with a lifespan of seventy or eighty years, only to then die and perish. But that is not who or what we are at all. In reality we are all individualized states of spiritual consciousness, each one of us evolving toward the ultimate expression of being, according to our kind—that is, unbroken eternal fellowship or union with God. But first we find ourselves beginning life in a spiritual condition comparable to being a seed or a lowly worm. In terms of consciousness this translates into Adamic, dis integrated, dualistic, fear-driven prodigals.

Curiously, however, instead of being born headlong into Adamic consciousness, our human experience often includes at least a flirtation with and knowledge of the consciousness of Eden or soul reintegration, temptation, and the decision to leave our Father's house as prodigals (escape from our own soul register). In most of us this flirtation with the consciousness of Eden is brief, fanciful, and incidental. In other words, while it may be a mystical part of our human experience, it is not yet viewed in the light of sustainable evolutionary fulfillment. Or to put it yet another way, it is not where we belong. Where we belong, according to the law of consciousness evolution, is right where we are—that is, in a world of spiritual darkness, misery, and death. We are bound by Adamic consciousness, because that is our spiritual evolutionary status at this point in time.

Eventually, however, the seed sprouts and becomes a tree, and the caterpillar enters a cocoon and is transformed into a butterfly. Likewise, eventually man too must evolve. The state of consciousness that we presently are (Adamic) will be shed, just like the worm's body, and a new consciousness will take its place.

What is the new consciousness of man? It is Eden—the return to the Father's house, the reintegration of our soul register. Thus planted within us is the awareness that this state of consciousness exists and awaits our evolutionary thrust.

What about temptation and the decision to abandon our soul register? Though most people are unaware of it, these events did occur in our consciousness. Thus their outcome was inevitable. In other words, our joining with the world of dis integrated souls was done as a matter of predetermined destiny, because that was the state of our consciousness evolution at that point.

As a matter of conjecture, we might even say that we were born into this world as a direct outworking of our state of Adamic consciousness—that it was a kind of placement based on the laws of creation and consciousness evolution. The planet earth was designated as the playground of Adam. Thus all those born into human life in a human body have come to earth to express Adamic consciousness for as long as it takes them to evolve. So it may be that our memory of Eden is a pre-birth memory carried in our consciousness and that our experiences of temptation and expulsion were pre-birth experiences that were actually the cause of our present placement.

In any case, conjecture aside, the important points to remember are these: we are not these human bodies or minds, but are individualized states of spiritual consciousness *with* human bodies and minds; we are not static or fully evolved, but are still in the process of evolutionary unfoldment; the consciousness embodied in the Adam mind is a darkened, lower state of consciousness, as expressed by willful soul dis integration and the temptation of prodigality; and finally, that the consciousness of Eden or soul reintegration awaits us as the next evolutionary step for our kind.

As has been well documented, there have been a few individuals born of our species that have transcended the consciousness of Adam while on this earthly plane and broken through to the new consciousness of soul reintegration. This experience by the few means that it is definitely possible for all human beings. It also means that it is our ultimate evolutionary goal. But clearly the collective condition and natural inclination of our species at this time is still Adamic or dis integrated. That is why human history has been and continues to be so repetitious and circular. Adamic consciousness is still the right fit for us. But as more and more individuals experience consciousness evolution, it will eventually change the collective chemistry. This change will then be reflected in the socio-political climate of the world, and history will no longer play itself out like a broken record.

Further Dynamics of Consciousness

Deep down we all know the truth about these dynamics of spiritual consciousness. It was to this innate understanding in his listeners that Jesus directed most of his teachings. That is why superficially his teachings often seem veiled or incomprehensible, and yet on some level of our inner being they make perfect sense.

To understand human life in the context of evolving spiritual consciousness is to know the truth that sets us free. To live as though spiritual consciousness is a non-factor in our human experience only reveals the extent to which we have been blinded by the Adam dream.

It is a fact that we have all abandoned our soul register and sought refuge in the world, as we now know it. The reason for this was the perception that the sin and uncleanness in our soul had become unmanageable and overwhelming. This uncleanness also involves karma because it reflects a carry-over and compilation of sins from past lives. So sin, guilt, karma, world mesmerism, emotional entanglement, and the sense of hopelessness these evoked in us compelled us to flee. What we refuse to recognize and admit to ourselves is the role that temptation played in this decision. We not only felt overwhelmed by our soul's uncleanness, but also were tempted to leave by the lure of prodigality. This is because we perceived that our state of consciousness was more harmoniously aligned with the world of men than it was with the activity of God in the kingdom of heaven.

Adamic consciousness, as prophesized in the Parable of the Garden, manifests as the essence of prodigality. We call it independent initiative, and we tend to glorify it even now after centuries of evidence that its effects are actually execrable. This glorified prodigality lures us away from our own soul register. True, the situation there appeared rather hopeless, but we conveniently overlook the option of giving God a chance to help us. We forget the scriptural truth that with God all things are possible, because according to the temptation of Adam, we are itching to be separated from God and determined to make our own way. That is the mystery of temptation at work in us, and that is why our world is like it is—that is, a world of soul less prodigals, seven billion strong.

Only after we have embraced the world and drunk the cup of its emptiness and cruelty to the dregs, do we think about our disenfranchised soul and the possibility of God helping us to return there. Prior to this it seems inconceivable to think of leaving the world and moving back into our soul register. Our entire life has been one long investment in prodigal initiative and escapist incentive. Any memory we have of pre-prodigal reality is so hazy that we tend to view it as fantastical. But it is through consciousness evolution that we grow beyond such stunted viewpoints and become amenable to the idea of return. Therefore it is consciousness evolution that also gives us the impetus to carry it through.

The world of men is a world of soul less human beings, pretending to live meaningful lives by busily filling their time and inner vacuum with intellectual and emotional stimulation. But this pretentious busyness does not change the fact that people are only half there, half alive. Without access to their soul register, people exist only as shadows. They have no anchor, no substance, and no solidity. They are essentially filled with vacuous space. This is the state of consciousness we have become comfortable with, but it is not our ultimate created potential. We were created to inhabit our soul realm, be fully integrated, and enjoy unbroken fellowship with God.

This is where the mystery of temptation subverts us, however. Does the world admit to being a soul less shadow land? Of course not. Rather it paints a picture of itself as being a sort of paradise in its own right, despite obvious appearances to the contrary. This is called living a lie. And the world has been passing this lie off as truth for so long, it has finally come to be fully accepted and believed in by all. Therefore knowing the truth about the world is imperative. And the way we come to know this truth is by beginning to see by the light of consciousness evolution.

The key to knowing all truth is the delineation of states of consciousness. Only in this way can we dispense with judgment, condemnation, and negative emotionalism. In other words, when we understand the human predicament in the light of consciousness evolution, there can be no condemnation or blame. The fact that we chose soul dis integration for ourselves instead of trusting God is not condemnatory; it is destiny based on the alignment of our present state of consciousness.

This is what made Jesus' teaching so compassionate. He knew how important it was for men to know the truth. In fact, he once stated that it was for this purpose—to testify to the truth—that he had been born into this world. (John 18:37). But he also saw plainly that men were not to blame for their predicament, since it was a matter of spiritual consciousness alignment.

None of this is meant to absolve us of personal responsibility in these matters, however. What is that responsibility? It is to respond to the evolutionary impulse to embrace the new consciousness, when its time has come. And that time is now.

For six thousand years we have been living an experiment of prodigality. Like the younger son in Jesus' parable, we have all left our Father's house (our own soul register) in response to the temptation of willful separation and independent initiative. Then as an expression of the Adamic consciousness we embraced, we joined our fellow soul exiles in the world of men. The life we have forged for ourselves in this world is a reflection of the Adam mind—that is, the mind of sin, separation, duality, and emotionalism. We all know what this life entails. We all have experienced it and languished in its sufferings. But there comes a time when the prodigal son comes to his senses, or in terms of consciousness evolution, is ready to move on to a new way of seeing and experiencing. He is ready to leave his life of Adamic torment and suffering and return to his Father's house. Though this sounds like he was going backwards instead of forwards, he was actually leaving behind a state of consciousness that was small and dark in favor of one that was more expansive and full of light. Adamic consciousness was once the right fit for him, but eventually he outgrew it. His coming to his senses was nothing more than the recognition of his readiness to move on. And acting upon this recognition was his personal responsibility being fulfilled.

There was no condemnation for the prodigal son's decision to leave, and there was no judgment upon his return. In fact, he found only unconditional love awaiting him. It was the Father's position simply to wait—wait until his son had evolved enough in consciousness to where he desired to return. This same waiting is called for in the evolution of plants, as they grow from seeds into fruitful trees, and for insects as they morph from worms into beautiful winged creatures. The Father is perfectly amenable to waiting, because He sees the bigger picture. In the light of consciousness evolution He sees that the actual evolutionary thrust of any creature is an already established fact.

But let us not lose sight of this: the prodigal son *did* eventually come to his senses; he *did* take full responsibility for the mess he had made of his life; he *did* take the initiative to return, even though he could not be sure how his Father would receive him. Perhaps all this was possible for him on account of how much he had suffered. In any case, what was plain was that his consciousness had evolved beyond the egoistic attachment to independent self-initiative that is the essence of prodigality. He was ready for greater spiritual light.

Clear Seeing

It is entirely possible then to vanquish the sense of mystery and confusion surrounding human life forever. But in order for clarity of mind to descend, we must first experience the soul reintegration that is the essence of the new consciousness. Prior to this evolution of consciousness we will be blinded at least to some degree from seeing the truth. The heavy emotionalism of the Adam mind will keep us incessantly agitated and off balance and render our intellectual attempts at achieving clarity as inconsequential. The New Testament calls this *seeing through a glass darkly*, while the clear seeing alternative is alluded to as *seeing God face to face*. (1 Corinthians 13:12).

If we are shut out of our soul register we are essentially fragmented in our human psyche. Therefore whatever knowledge we profess to have will not carry any real power. It will be merely borrowed, without our own experience to back it up. On the other hand, once we are reintegrated, our knowledge becomes consistent and true. This was what the people who heard Jesus preach and teach meant when they said, "He teaches as one who has authority." (Luke 4:32). Jesus conveyed the truth about the kingdom of God as one who had experienced that truth in the depth of his being. He taught about the inner kingdom of soul as one who had been fully reintegrated and made whole. In contrast, the Pharisees taught the scriptural truth of the Mosaic Law, but their knowledge was merely borrowed because they were still locked out of their own soul registers.

When we return to our soul register we automatically begin to see things more clearly. This is because all of the gunk that formerly made the glass dark and impaired our sight has been removed. Coming home inwardly cleanses us from all of the lies and distortions of the world, and once we are thusly cleansed all of the world's muddying influences are soon forgotten. The beauty we behold and the complete provision we enjoy in our newly planted soul garden enable us to relax and cease from our intellectual labors. Being no longer compromised by our involvement with the world, we can safely withdraw from it and stop looking to it for answers. Lastly, as we begin to perceive reality as it truly is—that is, in terms of consciousness evolution—we become so confident in this new way of seeing that we soon forget all of the erroneous beliefs we had been entertaining while under the spell of the Adam mind.

With clear seeing comes added benefits that further strengthen us. One of these benefits is the sense of wholeness—of no longer feeling fractured or dis integrated. Suddenly it dawns on us that we are now home and fulfilled. We are harmoniously aligned with our creator and our created mandate. We have now entered the effortless flow of divine creation and the perfection of being. Therefore there is nothing more to strive for or attain, since oneness with God and experiencing soul reintegration represent the ultimate fulfillment for our species.

We also feel certain of the fact that we have now laid hold of eternal life. This realization sets us free from the most primal fear known to man—the fear of death. When we are free from the fear of death, we literally feel indestructible. Our soul garden becomes like a hiding place, where nothing can enter to defile or destroy. Nothing can harm us anymore. We need no longer fear what man can do to us. Therefore we can love our fellowman, regardless of his occasional hurtful intent. This is loving our enemy according to Jesus' difficult teaching. It is viewing our fellowman with compassion and seeing him as he really is—a desperate prodigal trying to fend for himself by aligning himself with the spirit of this world; a soul refugee who fled his own unclean soul register and succumbed to the deceitful lure of the world.

When we see clearly we leave behind all the misconceptions about God we had once entertained and clung to. We worship God in Spirit and truth in fulfillment of Jesus' description of the kind of worshippers God desires. (John 4:24). This could also be spoken of as the mastering of God science. And when we know God scientifically we then have the tools for unleashing Its healing and life-affirming activity throughout our inner world. God is impersonal, omnipresent, omniscient, omnipotent Spirit. Therefore the entire regimen associated with trying to influence a personal God to act on our behalf ceases. To know God as impersonal

Spirit is to elevate our own consciousness to the attainment of God union, and there can be no greater enlightenment for us than that. To worship God in Spirit and truth is to enjoy pure unbroken fellowship with divinity throughout eternity.

The creation of God is spiritual in nature and quality. Contrary to what we perceive with our conditioned human senses, there are no evil or aberrant forces at work in God's creation. Rather all was created and is sustained in the perfection of being.

All that was created by God maintains a spiritual connection with God, and God, as Spirit, inhabits every nook and cranny of Its creation. Therefore all of creation is one with its maker and one with each other. There are no such things as divisions, dualities, or competitive opposites. There is only harmony, only oneness. The Adam mind is a misperceiving mind. The proof of this is that as soon as the madness of the Adam mind is cast out and clear seeing is restored, what we then see is the interconnectedness of all created life. When this happens, it is not God doing something new. Rather it is that we are finally perceiving things as they really are and always have been.

As a species we take great pride in our intellectual prowess—that is, the ability to discern between good and evil. But this entire mindset—the mind of Adam—has been shown to be faulty. Even the good is tainted, because it is measured against a non-existent evil. Meanwhile God is in Its kingdom, and God is one.

The Tree of Life

"The Lord God made the earth and the heavens. . . .The Lord God planted a garden in Eden, and there he put the man he had formed. . . .The Lord God made all kinds of trees grow out of the ground—trees that were pleasing to the eye and good for food. In the middle of the garden was the tree of life." (Genesis 2:4,8,9). This parabolic description in the Book of Genesis is prophetic of the experience of consciousness evolution or soul reintegration. As such, it dispels all sense of mystery and confusion about human life.

When we are moving in the consciousness of Adam, there is no God in our experience—no creator, no garden, no divine pleasure and provision, and no eternal life. What is there? The world of men—that is, a world created by the human mind, in which we collectively adhere to the theory that man evolved biologically as a species, according to a haphazard universal placement that enables us to glean provision from the earth. We ourselves mold this environment; we ourselves derive pleasure from our experience, if any is to be had; and we ourselves see to our provision—one that we invariably make happen by the sweat of our brow. Then after seventy or eighty years of this, we die. This is the Adam dream, and it has nothing whatsoever to do with the kingdom of God. But as we evolve in spiritual consciousness and are reintegrated in our soul, the Adam dream is shattered and the Genesis story of creation begins to make sense. Many of the things we once believed suddenly appear almost nonsensical.

One of the first beliefs we throw out the window is the preposterous notion that our species evolved from some lower form of primate. Until we gain the modicum of spiritual truth that God exists and that we were created alongside every other living creature on the earth, our entire perspective of the universe will be out-of-whack. The origin of human life was not just some arbitrary accidental biological event. It was purposeful, intelligent, and benign. Human survival has never been dependent on our own cleverness and strength. It has always been in the hands of God—the one-life, one-power that created and sustains us. The only evolutionary impetus that pertains to man is the evolution of spiritual consciousness. This is indicative of our high-created estate. We did not evolve from apes. We were created as human beings with spiritual consciousness. Apes have no spiritual consciousness whatsoever. But human beings have two potential spiritual evolutionary plateaus—Adamic or human self-realization and edenic or higher Self-God realization.

Next to be ascertained is that one of God's primary attributes and activities is that of redeemer or soul-cleanser. God is life eternal; God is the perfection of being and always manifests as spiritual harmony; God is our provider—an attribute that accompanies the work of creation. And God is a God of spiritual redemption, bringing cleansing and purity to all It touches. This is spoken of in the biblical parable as the activity of planting a garden. God not only created us, but then God planted a garden in Eden—that is, our soul register. This garden planted in our soul is the perfection of beauty and purity. It signifies the end of sin, guilt, karma, world mesmerism, and emotional entanglement in our life experience. Its beauty and perfection speak of fulfillment, wholeness, and completeness. In other words, if God has redeemed us—that is, planted a garden in our soul and put the man in it— we are home. There is nothing more to attain to or accomplish. In the New Testament this is called *entering the Sabbath rest of*

God. It is the next plateau in our collective spiritual consciousness evolution.

In the middle of the garden that God plants in our soul is the tree of life. Its central location speaks of this tree's central importance in our spiritual consciousness evolution. God is life. Therefore Its activity in our inner world is life affirming. And this life is not to be confused with our human version of an eighty-year lifespan that ends in death. That human experience is only an appetizer for God's true life, which is eternal-resurrection life.

The fact that this gift of life is to be found in God's garden means that it is also an aspect of God's redemptive principle. Without our consciousness releasing God's activity in our inner world, there would be no redemption for our soul register and no possibility of soul reintegration. We would still be *in our sins*. There would be no garden planted and no invitation to return. Thus there would be no eternal life. This is why Jesus stressed the need for redemption and the forgiveness of sin above all other facets of his ministry. It also explains why he alluded so often to his purpose being that of bringing eternal life to men.

God is the creator of the earth and the heavens and everything in them. The tree of life is planted by God in the midst of the redeemed soul. Only when human beings evolve in spiritual consciousness can they ascertain these realities. In the Adam world it is a stretch for us to even believe that God exists. No wonder the idea of eternal life is viewed as nothing more than a wishful fantasy. But when our spiritual consciousness begins to stir and expand in response to evolutionary impulses, we will be on our way to realizing God in every facet of Its being—first as extant, second as creator, third as provider, and fourth as redeemer.

Wherever God is there grows a magnificent garden. Whatever God touches becomes imbued with life and grandeur. In God's presence the barren field becomes a forest; the human body ravaged by disease is restored to perfect health; the problem of supply dissipates; and the human soul is cleansed of all sin, guilt, karma, defilement, and entanglement. Therefore there is nothing else that we need to do, other than to realize God's presence within us. For, it is our realization of God's presence that causes God to become active in our individual experience.

Chapter Nine

God Consciousness

Though rarely spoken of in such blatant terms, we live in a society in which many people harbor a profound antipathy toward God. Not surprisingly then, we encounter this same dynamic at work in the collective psyche toward the evolution of spiritual consciousness. Or for some, the idea of higher consciousness evolution might be palatable, but only if God is left out of it. Unfortunately, this is not doable, anymore than you can separate the wood from the tree. You cannot leave God out of Its own creation. You cannot leave God out of spiritual consciousness, because spiritual consciousness *is* God consciousness.

God is Spirit, and God union or the attaining of Spirit oneness is the ultimate goal of consciousness evolution. The highest evolutionary plateau known to us at this point is God union. So the new consciousness very much involves God. This is the rock of offense that causes many to stumble.

Unless we can resolve the *God question* then, our progress toward the light of the new consciousness will balk. How do we do this? We ask ourselves: what is it about God that disturbs us? Then ultimately we need to divest our minds of all our former concepts, until we can see God in a fresh new light.

Many people in western society have had negative religious experiences, some of which date back to early childhood years and are therefore a source of psychological conditioning against God. This does not imply that these conditioned concepts must remain entrenched in our psyche forever. It only means that for those who have them it will take a little more effort to dig them up and root them out. Amazingly, just this process of *unlearning*, if approached with diligence and determination, can work a true wonder in our lives.

At the root of most erroneous beliefs about God is the idea that God is a personal being who, though powerful, is subject to mood changes, caprice, dualities, and emotional upheaval, just like a man. This concept of anthropomorphic personalization may facilitate our ability to relate to God, but invariably a relationship built upon such a dynamic, like most human relationships, will suffer setbacks in the realm of misunderstanding, disappointment, miscommunication, and misperception. Then in the worse case scenario it becomes dysfunctional. And when that happens, we often decide we do not want anything further to do with God.

The question to ask ourselves at that juncture is: was God really to blame for this falling out, or was it the fact that I had a wrong concept about God in the first place?

What if God is not a personal being at all? Just entertaining such a possibility can be the impetus for life-changing healing and forgiveness. For if God does not become personally involved with us, then It could not very well have done those things to us that we imagined It did. Thus the truth that sets us free is that God is not like a man after all; rather God is impersonal Spirit.

God never withholds, never curses, never condemns, and contrary to most biblical interpretations, never judges. God is only good. God is our creator, our nurturer, and our sustainer. God is our redeemer and healer. Why would we want to harden our hearts against a God like that?

We were created to have fellowship with God—no, not an up-and-down emotionally volatile relationship, but pure effortless enjoyable fellowship. Thus the new consciousness not only includes God; it involves knowing, loving, and interacting with God. Though God is impersonal Spirit, it is possible for us to do this. It is a capacity we were created with. But it is up to us to get the ball rolling—first, by coming to know God aright and then by bringing our lives into harmony with God's law and created principle. God never changes, but our human consciousness must evolve to where we can exercise the faculty of spiritual discernment.

Spiritual Discernment

Coming home to our individual soul register is synonymous with coming home to God. Soul reintegration is a state of spiritual consciousness evolvement that promotes the development of spiritual discernment. What is spiritual discernment? It is the ability to perceive with a sixth sense—that is, to perceive spiritual realities that are imperceptible to our five bodily senses. Prior to experiencing soul reintegration we will perceive God as though through a glass darkly. But after we are settled in our soul garden we will see God face to face. We will walk with God in the garden in the cool of the day. (Genesis 3:8).

It is God that adorned our soul register in preparation for our return. God planted a garden in our soul and wooed us back from our hurtful prodigal exile. God made all kinds of trees grow in our garden—trees that were aesthetically pleasing and fruitful for nourishment. And in the middle of the garden God planted the tree of life, so that we need never fear death again. God did all this for us out of love, because that is God's nature. Wherever God is, there is redemption and purity. Wherever God goes, a garden grows in that place. Therefore the greatest gift that God has to give is Itself.

To know God and have fellowship with God is what Jesus called eternal life. The Kingdom of God to which he often referred in his teachings is none other than the redeemed human soul register. God is present in Its kingdom at all times and in all areas. As Spirit, God not only inhabits Its kingdom; It permeates every facet. Therefore coming home to our soul register is tantamount to coming home to God—that is, to the realization of God's presence and the experience of God union.

Prodigality is the willful separation on our part from God's presence. Though God is everywhere or omnipresent, it is possible for us to cut ourselves off from that presence through an act of consciousness, just as it is possible for us to close the door to our soul register and walk away. Thus the state of human society is now and always has been a godless, soul less state. No activity or power of God can operate in such a climate of disbelief and denial. The entire concept of atheism is based on this apparent dearth of divine power in the affairs of men, when all the while it is we ourselves that have rendered God impotent.

As we sour on our prodigal misadventure, however, and begin to take steps back in the direction of our Father's house, we discover some very startling truths about God. First, we find that God is very much alive as a universal presence and that there never has been a time when God was not alive and present. But as impersonal Spirit, God is doing things according to Its own agenda. In other words, God never has been and never will be the puppet of human beings.

As we grow in spiritual discernment, little by little we come to recognize God's activity as a constant scientific universal force. It is then that we leave behind all of our error-prone ideas about God as a personal anthropomorphic being and cease from our futile attempts to influence and manipulate It.

Ultimately, as our revelations continue, we come to understand the true nature of God as wholly benevolent and loving and begin to experience these attributes in our lives in very real and practical ways. After experiencing God in these ways, we can never again doubt Its existence or intentions. When we have such assurances operating in our consciousness, then it can be said that we have attained at least a degree of God consciousness.

Spiritual discernment also teaches us to behold God's kingdom in the midst of a disbelieving world. Once our spiritual eyes are open, God's kingdom becomes as real to us as the kingdom of man, even more so. We see that God's kingdom has always been there in its full goodness and glory, but that we have missed it on account of our spiritual blindness. Our Adamic consciousness rendered clear seeing impossible. But embracing the new consciousness, in which we seek to live in a manner that is perpetually mindful of God's presence, opens our eyes fully to the beauty and perfection all around us.

Fellowshipping With God

Without question, the greatest emphasis of Jesus' teaching was that, thanks to God's redemptive nature and principle, there could never exist any real barriers between man and God. True, there could always be imagined barriers—barriers that we erect in our sinful minds. But Jesus labored tirelessly and furthermore suffered the anguish of the cross to show us that these barriers were insubstantial and flimsy. They had no law of God to back them up. They were only dark shadows in the minds of men— shadows of ignorance, superstition, and fear.

Thus spiritual enlightenment begins with this great discovery: fellowshipping with God is not only possible for us; it is our created birthright. All we have to do is to reject the belief that separation from God is desirous and binding. As a life orientation, this belief in our separateness is extremely harmful to us, for it completely violates our created mandate. Therefore the attaining of God consciousness also brings healing and eternal life. It is the ultimate outworking of our created potential.

What does it mean to have fellowship with God? How does one fellowship with Spirit? The answer lies in becoming mindful of God's presence, and this we do by becoming still and receptive in our consciousness. Thus it is expedient to have frequent personal times, in which we stop all other activities, get quiet, and focus our conscious awareness solely on the spiritual kingdom within us. This may not come easily at first, but as we persist eventually we will break through to a realm of silence wherein God's presence can be felt. Once we have broken through to that silent realm and experienced it, we will then be able to return to it at will. This conscious realization of God's presence in the silence, oft repeated, is the way we establish fellowship with God.

All this takes place as an act of our own consciousness. It has nothing to do with God's will or sovereign initiative. Like the father in Jesus' Parable of the Prodigal Son, God is content to wait for us, until it enters our heart to desire the reestablishing of fellowship. God is like a radio frequency. It is up to us to turn the dial, so that the frequency becomes clearly audible.

The other thing we come to understand is that God's presence is scientifically predictable in all matters of accessibility and nature. In other words, it is as sure as science that we will find

God when we search according to the right spiritual principles. Once we find God's frequency on the dial, we will not be in the dark about how to dial it up the next time. Once we know how to find God, God will always let Itself be found. It is also as sure as science that God's nature and activity will always be consistent and benevolent. That nature is full of power, but we need not fear God's power. It is the power to heal and give life, not to destroy and lay waste.

Making contact with God is never a matter of chance or even effort. It is a science based on the knowledge of spiritual principles. Our spiritual consciousness must first be developed to the degree that we experience soul reintegration. God is found only in our own soul garden—walking in the cool shade of the trees It planted. God is not found in the soul less world of men, so we might as well stop looking for It there. The kingdom of God is within us. Therefore we must go within.

What does all this say about the commonly held approach to prayer? First of all, if we have yet to be reintegrated in soul, our prayers will never reach God. They will never pierce the veil of human ignorance and wrong belief. Secondly, if we have experienced soul reintegration, prayer becomes superfluous. We realize then that there is no need to inform God of our needs and certainly no need to beg and plead. Rather if we are living in communion with God and harmony with Its law, God already knows our needs and is already seeing to their fulfillment.

Certainly God is to be worshipped, but true worship is born of knowledge and revelation. Jesus called this *worshipping in Spirit and Truth*. If we have come home to our soul register, we need no longer view God as remote or unreachable. We need no longer try to appease or placate God. We need no longer fear God. True, God is holy, but this holiness is an influence for good in our lives, not evil. It is a *peace-be-still* to all our wayward thoughts and emotions. In other words, we can stand in God's presence, holiness and all, once we ourselves have been redeemed and sanctified. And if we can stand with God, we will surely reap wondrous benefits.

Thus the fear of God is a misnomer. We who dwell in our soul garden and enjoy God's presence soon lose all fear of God. Even those who are at this time still locked out of their soul register and are aligned with the sinful world of men need not fear God. True, they will face many hardships, but it will not be on God's account. Rather it will be payback from the karmic law—the law of cause and effect. God is not a God of fear, but rather of love, redemption, and fulfillment.

Abiding in God

Jesus once said, "Abide in me, and you will bear much fruit." (John 15:5). Was he speaking of himself, the man Jesus? No, of course not. He was speaking of God as Spirit. Here then is the key to attaining God consciousness, which is ultimately the key to living life to the full. To attain God consciousness we must go further than knowing God aright, further than experiencing moments of fellowship and communion, further than adjusting our approach to prayer, and further than worshipping in Spirit and Truth. We must, as an act of our own consciousness, come to abide in and with God.

The word *abide* means *to remain or live with*. Thus it is a fulltime endeavor. There is no such thing as abiding part time or some of the time, as the fancy takes us. Abiding in God implies realized union with God—union of every facet of our being: mind, body, soul, and emotions. And since such union can never be accomplished by the exertion of human faculties alone, it must be done through an act of spiritual consciousness. In other words, it is not enough to will ourselves to abide in God. We must develop our spiritual consciousness to the degree that we realize union with God as an inviolable state of being.

How do we develop our spiritual consciousness? It was Jesus again who taught us the way, saying, "Know the truth!" Only knowing the truth concerning the activity of God in our soul realm will develop our consciousness. There are many "truths" out there floating around, but the vast majority of them will do nothing for us. Only the revelation that it is our own consciousness development that brings about union with God and the release of God's power will prepare us to abide in God. There are many devout lovers of God and Jesus, but most of them are missing this key. This can be seen by the lack of divine power and influence in their lives. Though they love God, they are still suffering the plagues of Egypt. But as soon as they happen upon this key truth and experience the consciousness development it invariably brings, almost overnight their lives are transformed.

Once our consciousness has developed to the point where God union is realized as spiritual truth, there is no longer any effort required of us to abide in God. The realization of oneness is so strong that never again can we view ourselves as separate.

Once the key to unlocking God's activity and power has been discovered, there will never again be a lack of power in our lives. Then Jesus' vision that we will bear much fruit will come to pass.

The key for us then is to develop our spiritual consciousness, and this we do through knowing the truth. Religious discipline can be a help, but only if it is based on the teaching of an enlightened master. Even with this, in many instances the truth of the master is twisted and misinterpreted, so that it is rendered ineffective. What this teaches us is that in order for us to have a realistic perspective of these matters, it is necessary to adjust our expectations and timetable. The fact is that for most people the development of spiritual consciousness is a long, sometimes life-long, pursuit—one that requires patience, equanimity, and perseverance.

Only as our spiritual consciousness develops are we able to realize God consciousness and abide fulltime in the Presence. Other forms of spiritual discipline may help to bring this eventuality to pass. But we must be careful not to cling to them. They are only stepping stones along the path, and as such, they have no inherent power of their own.

There is no true power in any human exertion, whether it be mental, physical, or religious. The only power is in the indestructible life of God. Therefore our only recourse to that power is to learn the God ordained methodologies for releasing it. Since God's kingdom is within us, Its power is primarily an inward phenomenon, which then works its way outward. Thus the release of God's power in our inner world is accomplished through the function of our own spiritual consciousness. And the key to that functioning is awareness or the ability to focus and abide, using all our created human faculties.

Conversely, the inertia that blocks us from abiding and releasing God's power in our inner world is caused by ignorance, unconsciousness, and fear. That is why the conditioned human mind is such a detriment to spiritual progress. It adheres to ignorance, persists in unconsciousness, and revels in fear. As simple as it sounds to develop our consciousness to where we can receive God's key and utilize it, our conditioned mind makes it very difficult indeed. Just take a moment and listen to your thoughts. Watch where your mind takes you. It is, in all likelihood, away from God.

The New Testament speaks of these dynamics thusly: "Be ye transformed by the renewing of your mind." (Romans 12:2). What does this mean? Stop thinking according to your conditioned mind's agenda. There is nothing good that comes from such thinking. It is only a fount of distraction, inertia, and resistance. Let your mind take on a new role—no longer as calculator and ruler, but rather as your servant and spiritual facilitator.

Spiritual consciousness and mind are closely related. We can use our mind to focus, abide, receive truth, and rehearse it. But only our spiritual consciousness is eternal. The proof of this involves our pre-birth existence. The only thread that connects us with our past lives is our spiritual consciousness. Meanwhile, when we are born we receive a new body and a new mind, and when we die these same faculties cease to exist. That is why so few of us have any memory of our past lives. Our spiritual consciousness has no such faculty, and our mind, while possessing the faculty of memory, only has the capacity to remember as far back as our birth, because that is all the experience it knows. With each new incarnation we receive a new body and a new mind. Thus this new mind knows nothing of our past lives, while our spiritual consciousness knows but has no faculty of memory.

Spiritual consciousness is the true master of our soul. Its foremost credential for assuming such an important role is found in its eternality or indestructible life. Mind is a human faculty that has run amok and passed itself off as the ruler of the human psyche. Its proper (created) place is that of a servant or aid to spiritual consciousness. Once this true order in our inner world is established, amazing things begin to happen in our lives.

Our individual spiritual consciousness is one with God. Thus God union need not be intellectually ascertained. It needs only to be spiritually realized. It is our conditioned mind's inflated sense of purpose and influence that turns God realization into a life-long pursuit. And ironically, most of our process consists of the steady and determined effort to strip mind of its former influence.

Spiritual consciousness is God consciousness. To exercise awareness of spiritual consciousness is to exercise awareness of God's presence. And to abide in the consciousness of God's presence is to release God's activity in our inner world. This is not a hit-or-miss proposition. It is consistent and predictable to a tee. Therefore it is rightly called by some *God Science*. In this sense God not only lets Itself be found by us, God lets Its power be scientifically deployed and depended upon.

— Jakeb Brock —

The gift of God to us is this divine ordination of law and principle. God did not leave us as orphans. It did not leave Its dealings with men to chance or uncertainty, and certainly not to whim or caprice. God is a rock of stability, strength, and trustworthiness, and the road to God realization is paved with divine assurance. God is eternal life. And we too will realize eternality the moment our spiritual consciousness receives the light of truth.

Chapter Ten

Obstacles to the New Consciousness

One of the most important questions that confronts us on the road to embracing the new consciousness is: Who was Jesus? How we are inclined to answer this question can either lead to a life-changing breakthrough in our consciousness development, or it can take us on an extended detour, upon which true forward progress is impossible. This is the sifting of the wheat and the tares that Jesus once referred to parabolically (Matthew 13:29,30). So it is likely that the mystery surrounding his persona and the use of this question as a winnowing fork was intentional on his part.

To know the truth about Jesus is the good seed that brings forth an abundant harvest, while to cling to a wrong belief about him acts like a weed that grows but is of no benefit and only takes up the soil. In this age both kinds of believers have been allowed to grow up alongside of one another, in order that they might reach maturity. Then it will be plainly seen in the day of harvest which plant is fruitful and which is only using the soil. So you can see that this is a very crucial distinction.

To worship Jesus as the one and only Son of God is a sure recipe for spiritual stagnation, for it causes us to ascribe all that he did and said to the fact that he was divine, instead of viewing it as pertinent to our own potential. Whereas if we see Jesus as one of many potential sons, then we open ourselves up to the spiritual growth and expansion of the new consciousness. When we worship Jesus and pray to him as God we attempt to invoke spiritual power vicariously. Then as we persist in this approach we become comfortable with it, in spite of the fact that our prayers go unanswered year after year.

Jesus never intended for us to worship him as God. That is something we decide to do all on our own cognizance, largely because it is one way to make sense of the vast disparity in spiritual consciousness between him and most human beings. The true teaching of the New Testament is that with Jesus as our *way-shower* we can and must aspire to have the same mind that was in him. We must aspire to the height of consciousness development that enabled him to heal the sick, raise the dead, and ascend to the Father in a cloud of glory. This is not only possible for us; it is, if we persevere in the truth, inevitable.

The new consciousness is nothing other than Christ consciousness, and, as such, it is no respecter of persons. It is the spiritual consciousness of realized God union. Jesus was a man who laid hold of this high state of consciousness, but this same high state can also be attained by you and me. It is the power of the Holy Spirit that achieves this and then works through us, just as it did through the man Jesus. This means that God alone is to be worshipped and glorified, not the man or woman who becomes the vessel and instrument for that glory. How is God to be worshipped? By knowing the truth that God is omnipresent, omnipotent, omniscient, impersonal Spirit and emptying ourselves of our personal egoic human identity, in order that our lives might be brought into harmonious alignment with God's perfect law and creative principle of being. This was what Jesus did. Was he unique or set apart? Of course he was, but not on account of some innate divine aspect in his makeup. Rather it was because so few other men have allowed themselves to be thusly used of God.

And so we acknowledge that there are some very tangible and tenacious obstacles keeping us from embracing the new consciousness. Worshipping Jesus as God is not only an obstacle; it is also an indicator that we have yet to get serious about our spiritual consciousness development—that we are skirting the responsibility of spiritual growth by seeking to live vicariously through a savior-figure. For most of us this is a belief we have accepted by way of false teachings. We fancy that worshipping Jesus is humbling and ennobling for us, when in truth what it appeals to most is our natural inclination toward spiritual sloth and inertia.

Even when we begin to get serious to the point that we gain the revelation of Jesus as way-shower instead of a do-all savior, we will not find the path easy. Jesus called this phenomenon the *cost of discipleship.* He taught that all men and women, regardless of race, religion, or language, were capable of embracing the new consciousness and doing the works he was doing. But he also taught that the way was narrow, and only a few would have what it takes to enter.

The Teaching of the Cross

Another major obstacle to the development of spiritual consciousness is the continuing catering to that unspiritual part of our human makeup that wants to be in control—the ego. The human ego is a very deceptive mental construct, which we all, in our ignorance and unconsciousness, have come to identify with as our core self. We build it up through mental conditioning and then watch as it becomes entrenched and enthroned in our inner world. Indeed for most of us our ego is king, and its dictates are beyond challenging.

So it is that when a modern man or woman considers the idea of self, it is their ego that they envision. But in truth this is a very poor excuse for a self. It is by nature corrupt, exploitive, highly insecure, temporal, and inexorably manipulative. Since the ego is a creation of our own mental processes, it can never be spiritual or eternal. It can neither discern nor be subject to spiritual truth. Its place is strictly out in the world of men, where it serves us as a sort of identity prop that gives us purpose and protection in that dog-eat-dog setting. Not surprisingly then, we find ourselves clinging to the sense of identity that our ego gives us and trying to apply that same sense to spiritual matters. Unfortunately, this is not only impossible; it is a blatant impediment to spiritual consciousness development.

Countless people have made this mistake, only to find that spiritual life is both unaffected by and off limits to ego. They were attracted to the things of God but were unwilling to let go of their attachment to ego. In line with spiritual principles, they were amenable to the idea of disciplining ego and trying to bring it into service to God, but it is here that ego exposes its deceptive quality. It pretends to go along with a new spiritual agenda and promises to do its best to facilitate our religious goals and aid in making us a better person. But all the while its true motive is that of insuring its own survival and dominance. As soon as it gets the chance, it once again exerts its mastery over us, thereby making us know that no true progress on our spiritual journey has taken place.

The inescapable fact is that ego has no place in our spiritual consciousness development. Its input is completely unsolicited and undesired. Let me repeat that for emphasis: *no ego!* Zip, zero, zilch. The new consciousness is purely spiritual. It has nothing to do with improved human hood or flawless displays of morality. The ego can and will adjust to a *religious demeanor.* This can be seen in the behavior of the Pharisees of Jesus' day. Their righteousness exceeded that of other men, but it was a righteousness that included the influence of ego. It was highly religious and moral, but in terms of spiritual consciousness development, it was nothing but a roadblock.

Jesus' teaching about ego was unequivocally clear. He not only referred to its unspiritual nature in his words and parables. He also demonstrated it through his choices and actions. It was such a crucial and central aspect of his teaching that he was even willing to die on the cross in order to show the necessity of leaving the ego out of the spiritual equation. Thus he seared the collective consciousness of man with the imagery of his cruel unjust death for two millennia.

Did Jesus die on the cross to his ego so that we do not have to die to ours? God forbid. Rather as our way-shower, he died to his ego so that we would understand the imperative to die to ours and not make the mistake of trying to carry our ego into spiritual pursuits. He died to his human ego on the cross and was raised as an ego less spiritual being of light in the resurrection. And so must we pick up our cross and follow him, if we hope to come into the light of the new consciousness.

What does picking up our cross entail? Jesus stressed this teaching with two words: *deny yourself.* What does it mean to deny one's self? It is to die to our ego. But be careful here. The cross is a final solution, without mitigating influences or compromises. To deny oneself does not mean to become less selfish or more willing to do for others. That is a deception of ego aimed at insuring its own survival. Remember that ego does not care whether one is worldly or religious. It does not care whether you are altruistic or self-absorbed. Its only real concern is survival. The teaching of the cross is not one of ego discipline or moral improvement; it is one of annihilation. The ego must die in order for the new consciousness to be resurrected in our hearts.

This subtle distinction between a greatly reformed and subservient ego and annihilation is what has kept the Christian Church in spiritual darkness for two thousand years. Even today the preaching from most Church pulpits reflects this error. They teach that we must sometimes deny ourselves—that is, our own wishes and desires. And they certainly harp at parishioners about the need for moral improvement. But they refuse to annihilate ego and put a total end to its influence. They cut it back to a stump, but they fail to root it out.

This mandate of annihilation is alluded to in the Old Testament also. When the Israelites took possession of the Promised Land, they were told to utterly annihilate all the people dwelling there at that time, lest their pagan practices became a snare to them. But in almost every instance the Israelites fell short of carrying out this command. They allowed a degree of pagan culture to survive, even if it was only a tiny, seemingly insignificant aspect. They balked at the idea of total annihilation and judged it as being too harsh and severe. They allowed the stump of wrong belief to infiltrate their own pure law, and sure enough, over time that stump grew and became a snare to them.

In the same way ego will try to convince us that the cross does not involve total annihilation and that when Jesus talked about denying ourselves he was really just urging us to become better, less selfish human beings. It too will use the argument that a loving God could never promote such a severe notion as annihilation. "What kind of God would that be?" it would have us consider.

Nevertheless, when Jesus said, "Deny yourselves, pick up your cross and follow me," he *was* speaking in literal terms. Thus the teaching of the cross is nothing short of the teaching of ego annihilation. In light of how grossly these words have been misinterpreted, he might very well have added, "Be careful not to stop short. Be sure to finish the job. Do not let even a stump of ego's influence remain in your life, or it will surely become a snare to you."

When dealing with ego, often times we sincerely intend to uphold the command to annihilate it but end up falling prey to ego's deceptive pitiful ploys. Thus we allow ego's stump to remain rooted in the ground. How then can we insure that our intention to completely eradicate ego's influence in our lives is upheld? The key is diligence. This usually means that we must deny ourselves and pick up our cross, not once, not twice, but repeatedly. We must diligently apply self-awareness to this predicament. And we must be unyielding and unsympathetic. As difficult as it seems, we must drive in one nail after another and make sure that ego does not wriggle its way down from the cross. Eventually, if we remain faithful to this regimen, we will succeed. Ego will give up the ghost and cease to be.

Overcoming the World

For many on the spiritual path the vast social conglomerate we call *the world* can be a stumbling stone. This might not be the case, if the world were just an innocent haphazard gathering of human life. But unfortunately the world as a collective entity has sought to solidify its own survival agenda and deceptive methodology, much like the individual ego. In fact, it is safe to say that the voice of the world is even more of a force to be reckoned with on account of its unabashed use of propaganda and psychological conditioning. Being exposed to these methods of herding and control from birth allows it to gain deep inroads into our individual psyche. Then with fear as its henchman, the voice of the world effectually silences any inclination on our part to doubt or question its authority. Moreover, its agenda is clearly meant to take us away from the new consciousness. Therefore as with the deceptive ploys of the individual ego, it is not uncommon for us to succumb to this unspiritual directive and find ourselves unable to break free of its controlling influence.

Jesus' teaching about the world acting as an obstacle to the new consciousness can be found stated succinctly at the end of the sixteenth chapter in the Book of John: "In this world you will have tribulation. But take heart! I have overcome the world." According to the tone inherent in his choice of words, Jesus knew that the world could act as an obstacle on our path to spiritual fulfillment. It could exert a proactive resistance aimed at keeping us stuck. The question is: why? When we can answer that question we will understand better what Jesus was saying.

In light of what we have learned thus far about the new consciousness and our own journey toward soul reintegration the world of men can never again be looked at as just an innocent haphazard gathering of people. True, it is a gathering, but we must remember that every human being has a common spiritual history—that of willful prodigality. In other words, the world is comprised exclusively of individuals that have become disenfranchised from their own soul register. Each and every one living in this world has at some point in time (and it may have been in a past life) made the choice to shut the door to his or her soul register and walk away. Thus the world as we know it is made up of fractured, dis integrated people.

Now along comes a spiritual seeker who begins to question his or her place in this prodigal society. This is not to imply that they themselves were not at one time partakers in the prodigal mindset. Like all the people in the world, such spiritual seekers also made the willful decision to abandon their soul register and join the prodigal throng. The difference is that these soul exiles come to regret the choice they made and begin to yearn for soul reintegration. They repent to the best of their ability and in so doing embark upon the journey that Jesus referred to as *the return to the Father's house.* What happened to them to elicit this response of regret? They perceived the state of soul dis integration and separation from God to be a worse fate than dwelling in an unclean soul register had been. They also came to dislike what they felt from the hardened prodigals who had helped to build this world and staunchly supported its status quo perpetuation. Thus their experience in the world became one of tribulation and pain. Then to add to their distress, as their unhappiness became known, it sparked a dynamic of persecution from their fellow prodigals.

It is not so much out of spite that the world opposes us. Rather it is on account of its age-old history of indoctrination and psychological conditioning. A world that revels in its prodigality naturally opposes the things of God. Therefore the very idea of leaving the prodigal world and returning to the Father's house is ridiculed and scoffed at. The culture and social climate of the world have become the collective voice of prodigality. Herein lies the impetus behind its resistance to the new consciousness. The degree to which we have been indoctrinated into the world's culture is the degree to which we will experience opposition, not only from outward persecutions but also from inward restraints, such as fear, doubt, and cowardice.

The world's loss of innocence then is not due to some evil conspiracy by fallen angels. It is strictly bound up with its shared prodigal agenda. Throughout history men have been wont to defend their prodigal instinct and fend off any suggestion that it is this very instinct that is the root cause of their problems and difficulties. This defense has taken the form of a common world reality view—a reality view based not on truth but rather on the justification of their prodigal instinct. Then as a way of securing that this reality system is upheld from generation to generation, men devised strategies for the indoctrination of the masses. They learned that if they can systematically impose their reality view on an individual from the day of his birth, that individual would never have the fortitude to question or deviate from it. In our modern world this imposition takes various forms. It comes through culture, media, and yes, our educational system. Its aim is to make the world one united front of prodigal instinct. So to go against this strong tide of human initiative can be a daunting prospect to say the least. It can be done, but it is not an easy undertaking. Thus Jesus' admonition to *take heart*.

How did Jesus overcome the world? Certainly it was not with armies or legions of angels. No, the world itself has been unchanged for thousands of years. What then did Jesus mean by the word *overcome*?

Jesus did not view the world or any other power in our universe as a power that could rival the power of God. To him God was the only true power. There was no evil power to be overcome by a good power. Rather God was all and in all.

Jesus saw that the so-called power that the world wielded was only a shadow on the wall. It was only the psychological suggestion that men dare not oppose it. Therefore the overcoming of which he spoke needed to be inward and secretive. The world could not oppose what it could not comprehend. And what it could not and indeed refused to even try to comprehend was spiritual truth.

Thus everything Jesus did and said was aimed at exposing the world's reality view as a non-power. By countering the world's deceptive influence with spiritual truth Jesus overcame its inertia. He taught that the world needed not be an obstacle to spiritual consciousness development.

So how do we ourselves overcome the world so that it is no longer an impediment to the new consciousness? We follow Jesus' lead and seek to establish ourselves solidly in the truth of God. We do not fight the world or rail against it or even try to change it. Rather we quietly withdraw into our inner world and make the necessary changes there. Jesus became so strong in the truth that he willingly allowed himself to be crucified, knowing that God's life is indestructible and that therefore the grave would not be able to hold him. That is true overcoming.

Unfortunately for most of us, establishing ourselves in God's truth is no easy task. But with diligence and perseverance it can be done. Jesus cannot do it for us, but we can take heart that he was able to overcome the world and be strengthened by that realization.

Spiritual Evolution

We have seen how false teachings about Jesus and God can be an obstacle to the new consciousness and how the ego can deceive us and send us down one detour after another. We have also seen how world mesmerism can hold us back. But when push comes to shove, the greatest obstacle we have faced, especially as a collective entity, has been spiritual evolution. The inescapable fact is that as a species we have not embraced the new consciousness thus far for one prominent reason: we have not been ready for it.

Everything in life hinges on spiritual consciousness development. Individually there is nothing stopping us from pursuing this goal, but collectively we have only been able to evolve at the pace of our weakest link. The question then that must be asked is: who or what represents our weakest link?

At first, in judging by appearances, we might be inclined to focus our attention on the more unseemly strata of human society—the poor, the sinful, the downtrodden, the sick and dying, etc. But Jesus taught that in the spiritual realm these posed no hindrance to collective spiritual evolution whatsoever, but rather were in fact a blessing to our race. And this has been proven over and over again by individuals who rose out of this strata and made great strides in their own spiritual consciousness development. From where then has our collective inertia consistently issued forth? The answer is that it has not been the weak that have held us back; it has been the strong. Thus ironically, from a spiritual perspective it is the strong that have been humanity's weakest link. It is the strong that have been primarily responsible for our collective resistance to the new consciousness.

Who are the strong in human society? This cannot necessarily be gauged by outward factors, such as wealth, fame, or political clout. Rather it is foremost an inward quality and as such can often remain hidden and concealed. Spiritually speaking, a wealthy or influential man could theoretically be as meek as a kitten. No, the true strong among us are those who tenaciously cling to the status quo at all costs, because it is through this status quo system that they have derived their influence and prosperity. And when they are clever, these strong ones tend to conceal their status quo sentiments. They work behind the scenes, doing everything in their power to make sure that the status quo agenda is perpetuated and spiritual evolution kept at bay.

For many, one of the true mysteries about Jesus' behavior, as described in the Gospel narratives, is how harshly he opposed these strong ones in his own day. One reason for this was that he first needed to draw them out and expose their true motives and intentions. For, they, being exceedingly clever, had been working behind the scenes and deceiving the people. But were they more wicked than other strong men who had lived before them or in other lands? Of course not. The human impulse to cling to and defend the status quo is a spiritual one and is no respecter of persons. It has manifested in peoples from every corner of the globe and in every time period. It is a lower state of evolutionary consciousness that disregards God's spiritual presence and law and seeks to establish prosperity in the human ranks through strength, violence, and deception. Thus it is by its nature resistant to the light of true spiritual evolution.

Jesus opposed these weak links to spiritual progress in his midst in the hope that they might learn the truth concerning what they were doing and open their hearts to the light of the new consciousness. But even Jesus could not bring light to these darkened minds. Their reactionary plan to crucify Jesus successfully enabled them to retain their vice-like control over the collective entity. Even the power of the resurrection was rendered nil by their lies and propaganda. Thus we see that Jesus was unable to bring about a change in the collective consciousness. The most he was able to accomplish was the imparting of a greater inspirational influence for individuals seeking spiritual salvation. He was not able to break down our race's age-long resistance to the new consciousness, because the strong—our race's weakest link—opposed the spiritual evolution he came to promote with such vehemence.

This is not to say that the members of the status quo hierarchy of Jesus' day were not threatened by him or that they were certain of their continued dominance. On the contrary, they were most uncertain and insecure. They knew that Jesus had the power to utterly expose them and undermine their authority. This was made clear by the desperate quality of their choices and actions concerning him. But in the end they prevailed, and there is one main reason why: the people themselves were unwilling to fully embrace the truth that Jesus was teaching them. They embraced it to some extent, but what was being called for then, even as it is now, was a complete and total rejection of the status quo agenda. And this was not something they were ready to do. Whether out of fear or cowardice, the people were not prepared to stand up to the status quo hierarchy and say: *enough!* They were not able to cut through the lies and distortions and see that spiritual evolution would bring with it a glorious new day for all mankind. Thus they failed to thoroughly reject the status quo agenda and dethrone those who were living by it. The fact that the people of Jesus' day failed in this regard, despite basking in the light of his consciousness, portended the inevitability of there following another two thousand years of status quo futility for our world.

The people of Jesus' day had the power to stand up to and overthrow the status quo hierarchy in their midst, just as we have that power today. But they were not ready to take such a unified stance and instead allowed their messiah to be crucified and his movement of spiritual consciousness evolution to sputter, stall, and be forced underground. Two thousand years later not much has changed in this regard. We still act as though the status quo initiative is a power that must not be challenged. But is it really the power we think it is? No, in fact it is not a power at all. The only reason we view it as such is because we have been conditioned from birth and mentally programmed to reject the new consciousness as a sort of unrealistic fantasy. We have been trained to accept the status quo initiative as the one true reality.

The day we see this is the day that the new consciousness will descend upon the collective entity, like the descent of the dove-like Spirit of God. In that day it will be understood that the proponents of our race's age-long status quo sentiment have been our weakest link and that it was on account of their inability to evolve spiritually that the nightmare of soul less, God less human life lasted as long as it did.

Chapter Eleven

Coming Home

The first step for an individual who seeks to embrace the new consciousness is described by Jesus in his wonderful Parable of the Prodigal Son in these words: *he came to his senses.* (Luke 15:17). Then what follows is an act of return—that which has sometimes been called *repentance.* Actually however, repentance is only one aspect of the return journey for the human soul. Also as part of that journey we must develop our spiritual consciousness to where we can realize or have faith in or *feel* God's presence within us. Then ultimately we must receive the key of knowledge that releases God's presence in our inner world to become active on our behalf and reverse the devastations caused by the working of the Adam mind. That is the new consciousness in a nutshell. And this same journey of return applies to the collective entity as well as the individual.

What does it mean to come to our senses? It is first and foremost to realize that something we have once believed in no longer works for us. In the case of the prodigal son, after much suffering and deprivation he realized that prodigality or separation from the Father was a mistake; it no longer worked for him; its deceptive luster had worn off, and it had been exposed as nothing but a devastation machine, churning out one harmful effect after another. In our case, coming to our senses implies that we recognize the futility of the status quo initiative of our world and accept the fact that it no longer works for us. After much pain and suffering we finally are ready to admit that our decision to associate ourselves with the prodigal world of men was a mistake. Its deceptive luster has given way to a bleak soul less reality, while our inner world has come to reel under the constant assault of the devastations caused by the Adam mind.

Recognizing that we have all been a part of the collective prodigal dream of Adam—that we were in fact born into it and raised up in it—is helpful for blurring the boundaries between our individual and collective destinies. In other words, we all have an integral stake in the collective destiny, as dictated by our human birth. So we all can feel the link between our individual spiritual consciousness evolution and that of the collective entity. That is why when we experience coming to our senses as an individual, it pains us that that same experience is eluding the collective entity. It is also why the salvation of an individual soul, while glorious in its own right, is still somehow not enough. Truly, the entire purpose for individual enlightenment is that ultimately the collective agenda will be so impacted that it will follow suit. This has been the impetus behind the teaching of every enlightened master that has ever walked this earth. The new consciousness, in order to come to full fruition, must become a collective reality. Therefore coming to our senses and setting out on the journey of return must eventually become commonly held experiences.

With that being said, and having just read a chapter about the many obstacles standing in the way of spiritual fulfillment, how can we begin to turn the tide? Of course, each one of us can and must develop our spiritual consciousness individually through the learning of truth. But what are some of the steps that we can take as a collective culture coming into the light? How do we come to our senses as an entire race of beings? How do we collectively undertake the journey of return?

Going Inward

As a prodigal society in which each member has at some point in time made the decision to walk away from his or her own soul register, we have become an outwardly oriented people. In our attempt to distance ourselves from the uncleanness of sin and karma piling up in our soul register we have turned outward to such a degree that we have become essentially alienated and cut off from our own inner workings. Therefore one of the major shifts that needs to take place in the collective psyche is to once again learn to value and discern our inner capacity as human beings.

It is not that we can redeem ourselves or become reconciled with an inner condition that is irreconcilable. Only God holds the key to these miraculous interventions. But what we can do is to shift our orientation from outward to inward and recognize this as the divinely ordained order of harmonious human initiative.

God created human beings with the ability to make their own world. But there is an order and legal basis to our creative powers. This order is that human creative energy has an inward basis, which then flows outward into physical manifestation. To create a world we must begin with vision and imagery. Only after these inward powers have crystallized do we then bring their outward forms into manifestation. According to this creative pattern we notice then that the truly benign aspects of our manifested reality or world have been those that have been inwardly nurtured and well developed prior to our attempts to make them manifest, while most of its detrimental aspects have been hurried into manifestation for no other reason than that we have come to put more stock in the outward than the inward. Often times in modern life we attempt to bypass the inward visionary stage altogether and focus exclusively on the outward result. That is why much of human culture in today's world has become shallow and vain. Anything worthwhile in the outer plane must have a well-developed inner basis.

By cultivating the shift in orientation from the outward to the inward we will infuse our culture with new content and quality. What is more, we will pave the way for the new consciousness by focusing our awareness on the source and law of our being. The new consciousness is strictly an inward phenomenon. It is not concerned with outward manifestation, knowing that this will happen automatically according to divine law. Thus it is in our inner world that all change and growth must take place. Human beings are primarily inward creatures. In truth, our consciousness development is the only reality there is, because anything that takes place in the outer realm only exists as a manifestation of consciousness.

Part of our coming to our senses then is the realization that our obsession with the outward orientation has been a mistake. Nothing good can ever happen for us as long as we persist in this unlawful order. Only as we turn inward and return to the harmonious orientation we were created to have can good things begin to happen. Only after we learn to value our inner capacity will the new consciousness find the right environmental climate to flourish. It will then put down roots and spread out to the right and the left, eventually filling the whole earth.

God exists as an inward creative force. The kingdom of God is within us. The realization of the divine Presence takes place in our inner world. And the conscious awareness of that Presence, which releases the power of God, is an inward impulse. Subsequently, the wonderful works of God, as represented by the reversal of the Adam mind's devastations, also take place within us.

All of this applies to the collective entity as well. Our shallow, outwardly oriented culture must be infused with a new emphasis on inward pursuits. The Spirit of God within the collective human psyche must be realized and worshipped in Spirit and Truth. Our culture must become a habitation for God's Spirit and activity, instead of the idol-worshipping venue it is at present.

Saying No to the Status Quo

In the end, if there is to be hope for the collective entity of the human race, we must find the strength to say *no* to the status quo sentiment that has dominated human culture since time immemorial. This is indeed a revolutionary notion, but it need not spark a violent brand of overthrow or political upheaval. The key is to recognize the detrimental influence that the status quo has wielded and then to step out in the knowledge that it is not a power. Remember that such sentiment would have no inroad into the collective psyche whatsoever, were it not for its shameless employing of such mind controlling techniques as infantile suggestion and conditioning. Thus to stand up to the status quo will prove easier than we thought.

Until the time of the new consciousness has fully dawned and its light brightens the human stage like a sun, the status quo will still find a resounding chord in the hidden recesses of men's hearts. But what we can do until then is work to lessen its influence. This we do by exposing it repeatedly and relentlessly, as Jesus did. By doing this we essentially are demanding that all the captives—that is, the victims of the status quo's deceptive agenda—be released and set free. Then as more and more of these oppressed ones are set free to flower in the new consciousness, the influence of the status quo will gradually be undermined, until one day it is altogether vanquished.

Until the world of men undergoes these changes, we must make a conscious effort to distance ourselves from it. As the scripture exhorts: "Come our from her, my people, so that you will not share in her sins, so that you will not receive any of her plagues." (Revelation 18:4). Many make the mistake of thinking that such extreme measures are uncalled for. They think they can keep one foot in the world and point the other toward the spiritual kingdom. But in truth, such a stance only results in floundering.

The best thing we can do for ourselves *and* for the world is to leave it behind entirely. This elicits a testimony of spiritual power that the status quo cannot easily slough off.

The status quo sentiment includes the lie that not only does it express the true reality view; it also would have us believe that this reality view is inviolable and age enduring. Only when we leave the world of men behind can we break free of and refute such debilitating notions. Remember the status quo has an agenda of control that it is carrying out, and it will stop at nothing to see that agenda fulfilled. It will lie, distort reality, and try to strike fear into our hearts. It will make it seem that our dependency upon the world can never be doubted and that leaving it will lead to ruin.

But the truth is that we can and must separate ourselves. We can simply walk away and come out from her. And as we do this we find that it is not very difficult after all. It certainly is not ruinous. If anything, it has a strengthening and liberating effect upon us.

When the status quo hierarchy of his day hung Jesus on a cross and succeeded at rendering the testimony of the resurrection powerless among the masses, it gained a reprieve of two thousand years for the status quo in general, with which it could perpetuate its influence and keep the new consciousness at bay. But to call the status quo initiative *age enduring* is simply a lie. The status quo hierarchy throughout each generation has known this, and that is why they have never let up in their efforts at propaganda and mind control.

The truth is that the dawning of the new consciousness is inevitable and unstoppable. In the long run spiritual evolution will show itself to be an indomitable divine force, and when that happens the status quo sentiment that has characterized human experience throughout this age will dissolve.

The Perspective of Eternality

In truth, the world of men and everything in it is passing away before our eyes. How can this be? Because it is a strictly temporal phenomenon. It was not created by God and is not sustained by God. It is sustained only by human strength and ingenuity. True, it *appears* to be enduring, and those who have been conditioned by the status quo's propaganda machine have come to believe that this present world culture is the one enduring reality. But from God's perspective, ten thousand years of temporal human endeavor on the earth are like the blink of an eye. They are like a footprint in the sands of eternity—one that when it has been made leaves no lasting imprint.

From the perspective of eternity this world is passing away. As we abide in the truth of the new consciousness we gain this revelation: worlds will come and worlds will go, while we remain forever. Therefore we need not concern ourselves with the temporal world of men. Our only concern is to dwell with God in our soul garden. There we will find our sustenance and the perfection of life unto eternity.

Can we really remove ourselves from this world to such an extent that it no longer concerns us? Can we let it go its own way and cease to be moved by its suggestive agenda? Can we take the burden of worldly concern off of our shoulders? Yes, yes, yes, we can. Who then is there to be concerned about the plight of man? God alone. This means that if we are to become ministers of the new consciousness in this temporal world, it will only be because God's concern is moving us to do so. Thus we become God's ministers. But this commission in no way impacts our true perspective of eternality. We do not get lost in the temporal world again. Rather we continue to dwell in our soul garden eternally.

This is the fulfillment spoken of in the Book of Revelation as having perpetual access to the Tree of Life (Revelation 22:14). The perspective of eternity sets us free from the world, not only in regards to our false concerns, but also from its multitude of plagues and devastations. Thus the more we partake of the fruit from the Tree of Life, the more our spiritual consciousness expands and thrives.

The True Meaning of Prodigality

The new consciousness is a coming home to our true Self. When the temporal world of men was our world, we lived as prodigals. We were inwardly fractured and dis integrated. We suffered from all the plagues of Egypt and knew no peace.

What does it mean to be a prodigal? It is to willfully cut ourselves off from the divine Father-aspect of our being and shun our inheritance as the Son who has perpetual access to the Tree of Life.

Embracing the new consciousness is a journey of return. That is why we must leave the world. As a collective unit, it has not yet committed to taking that journey. Rather it is in a holding pattern, in which the status quo initiative continues to dominate and promote prodigality. As such, it is hopelessly temporal or passing away.

Prodigality was not forced on us. All of us at one time made a conscious decision to become prodigals. Our common experience has been one of being born into this world, in which the mind of Adam is dominant and controlling, thereby subjecting us to the psychological suggestion or brainwashing of Adamic culture. This post birth, infantile inundation brought sin into our personal experience, because the Adam mind *is* sin. And once sin began to pile up in our soul register, we then became ripe for the lure of prodigality.

What is the lure of prodigality? It is the idea that there is a human solution to sin and soul uncleanness. Of course, even prodigal society does not claim to have a method for doing away with sin. Rather its boast is that it lives free of the *effects of sin*, and the way it does this is by abandoning the soul register altogether or becoming a prodigal. Thus sin is not vanquished; it is only compartmentalized. The Adam mind still produces sin constantly, but as prodigals we no longer concern ourselves about this. We let our sin pile up behind the closed door of our soul register and forget about it.

This is how the world of men operates. That is why God is not in it. Meanwhile the proponents of the status quo have committed themselves to perpetuating the godless, soul less climate of this world for as long as they can, to the degree that they have put forth a completely false and fabricated testimony about how well prodigality fits the human race. Shamelessly, prodigal society has portrayed itself as the ultimate expression of human ingenuity and fulfillment. With sin no longer a pressing issue, dedicated prodigals will testify that they are able to live freely and happily. Inherent in their doctrine is the idea that soul reintegration is overrated and unnecessary. What is important is being able to live freely, without the constraints of an obsessive awareness of sin. Therefore the lure of prodigality is bound up with this false testimony. All of us who came to a place of feeling helpless and hopeless with the unclean condition of our soul register fell for this false prodigal testimony hook, line, and sinker.

Thus we too abandoned our soul register. We too shut the door and walked away. We too saw prodigality as the answer to the sin problem. We too accepted the idea that soul reintegration was overrated and unnecessary. And we too were eager to give prodigality a chance to succeed. But unlike the upholders of the status quo, our experience in prodigal society did not result in a wholehearted allegiance to it. Rather something about it did not sit well with us.

Perhaps it was the sense of our own disconnectedness and dis integration that troubled us. Perhaps it was seeing the truth about our fellow prodigals—that they were not as happy and fulfilled as they pretended to be. Perhaps it was the Darwinian climate of prodigal society—the fact that everyone was in it for themselves and there was neither help nor mercy to be found there. Whatever the case may have been, something went sour for us, and we began to regret our choice. This was the point, wherein we began to come to our senses.

What followed was a journey of return that was both long and arduous. What made it so difficult was the thought that once we did find our way back to the door of our soul register, what then? How could we expect to find things any different in that realm than they were before we gave in to the lure of prodigality? Our soul uncleanness—the reason we had left in the first place— would not have magically disappeared. In fact, if anything the situation had probably gotten worse. Our sins and karma had continued to pile up while we were gone, and now in all likelihood that pile had become a mountain.

On our journey of return we learned the truth about God and our own inner makeup. We followed Jesus as our Way Shower and gained a degree of spiritual discernment. Eventually we came to where we could perceive and feel God's presence within us as Spirit. We even received the key to unleashing God's healing power and activity in our inner world to counter and reverse the lifelong devastations of the Adam mind—the low life levels leading to death, the bodily dysfunction leading to disease, and the supply problems that resulted in an abiding sense of lack and limitation. But still we had not found the solution to sin, and therefore had yet to even attempt to reclaim our soul register. That door had remained shut.

Redemption: the Key to Soul Reintegration

Then one day it dawns on us that maybe God—the spiritual Presence within us—holds the key. So we ask, "Lord, is there anything you can do about the uncleanness in my soul register? I long to be able to reclaim my soul, but sin and karma have been having their way with me since my birth." "Of course," comes the

Lord's pragmatic response. "I have only been waiting for you to ask. Fear not. I am your redeemer."

Without further ado, God opens the door to our soul register. Stepping inside with Him, we see that our fears were fully justified. Just as we had thought, the devastation and putrefaction of sin piling up in our soul throughout the years of our prodigality were terrible to behold. Our own soul had become a barren wasteland, a haunt of jackals. Sin and uncleanness had become like an unmovable mountain. "Do not be dismayed," the Lord says, perceiving our disbelief and hopelessness. "I say to this mountain, 'Up with you and be gone.'" And with that a great miracle takes place. The mountain of sin disappears before our eyes. And with it our guilt is removed as far as the east is from the west. Not a trace of sin or guilt can be found remaining. Then walking a little ways we come to the karmic wheel. But strangely, the wheel has ceased its loud churning, and all is blessedly quiet. Looking down, we notice that the stream of uncleanness and sin entering our soul from past lives has stopped flowing and dried up. "What has happened here?" we ask the Lord. The answer comes: "The karmic wheel only operates in the absence of redemption. As soon as I entered your soul with my redemptive presence, it shut down." From there we walk to where a door stands ajar, flapping in the breeze. It is the door to friendship with the world that we had opened years before. At its base is a putrid stream flowing through—the stream of world mesmerism. Gently, the Lord shuts this door, and as He does so the stream ceases to flow and dries up to nothing. "Keep this door shut," God tells us. "Do not let the idea of friendship with the world deceive you. There is no help to be found there." Finally we approach a human figure that resembles us, except for the fact that this figure is tied up with several strong cords that seem to be choking the very life out of it. "What is the meaning of this?" we ask the Lord. "What is the meaning of these cords?" "These are the cords of emotional entanglement with others that you had allowed to take root in your soul and bind you. They too were a source of uncleanness for you."

With that the Lord's redemptive work in our soul register is complete. "Behold you are now clean," He pronounces. "Your soul has once again been made habitable. You are free to come home."

"What about sin Lord? How shall we keep sin at bay and avoid the return to an unclean soul condition?"

"I am now with you unto eternity. My redemptive presence in your soul will shield you from sin from this time forward. Whenever your Adam mind controls you and produces sin, that sin will not be able to attach itself to you. My redemptive presence will immediately cleanse you. Thus you never need to close the door to you soul register again."

And so it is that we experience soul reintegration through the new consciousness. We leave behind the prodigal world of fractured dis integrated humanity and come home to our Self. We take up residence within our newly cleansed soul, and this residency is never again in jeopardy because God's redemptive presence dwells in us. No longer are we vulnerable to the lure of prodigality. At last our journey of return is complete.

The New Consciousness and Jesus

All of a sudden it makes sense to us why the main thrust of Jesus' ministry was redemptive in nature and why soul reintegration was such a priority in his teaching. Thanks to Jesus, God's redemptive nature not only became known; it became freely accessible and operational. In this way Jesus became the foremost advocate of the new consciousness in this age.

The new consciousness is all about redemption. Its emphasis is on union with God—a union so complete that we lose all sense of individual self and merge into the one Greater Self, which we call God. This is the parabolic teaching behind Jesus' cross and resurrection. Our small temporal self (ego) must go the way of the cross in order for us to be resurrected as eternal unified God-Spirit.

The Adam mind—sometimes referred to as the *sinful mind* in scripture—is the mind of the pre-cross human self. It is this mind that is the source of all soul uncleanness—the soul condition that makes us vulnerable to the lure of prodigality and leads to disintegration. Conversely, redemption is the power or activity of God that cleanses us and neutralizes sin's effects, thereby enabling us to reintegrate and come home.

Was Jesus' ministry a success? Very much so. The status quo may have retained control over the world of men, but Jesus imparted to us a revelation of divine redemption that has never tarnished or faded. In this way he paved the way for the new consciousness and set in motion an indomitable outcome for human spiritual evolution.

Spiritual evolution has two aspects: individual and collective. Over the past two thousand years countless individuals have laid hold of the new consciousness through the vehicle of messianic redemption or the divine decree of forgiveness of sin. Nothing has been able to impede or stop this individual evolutionary thrust. But on the collective stage we have been held back by the status quo's deceptive impetus. Even now individuals continue to come into the light of the new consciousness everyday. Thus the spiritual power Jesus set in motion has proven to be indomitable.

Where will it all end? This question is not difficult to answer. Consciousness evolution will ultimately win out. That is the message of the resurrection. The status quo may be able to hang the new consciousness on a cross, but it can do nothing to stop the resurrection from taking place.

As evidenced by his marvelous miraculous deeds, Jesus not only advocated the new consciousness; he demonstrated it. In other words, he lived it. Therefore it is readily apparent that he could have prevented the status quo hierarchy of his day from hanging him on a Roman cross. But he allowed himself to be crucified for two reasons. One reason was that he did not want to deprive the world of the most poignant parabolic teaching about spiritual life that has ever been given, and the other was that he knew the world was not yet ready for the new consciousness. In terms of spiritual consciousness evolution it needed more time. So he left us for the time being and promised to return when the time was right.

Does this imply that the man Jesus will once again walk the earth? It is possible, but more likely is the scenario that the Spirit Presence or Christ which the man Jesus had fully realized within himself will this time become prominent and active on earth in the lives of Jesus' brothers—that is to say, humankind. This movement of the Christ Spirit will spur thousands and perhaps hundreds of thousands or even millions on to a condition of spiritual consciousness development that will be very much akin to Jesus' state of consciousness. These little Christs (the true meaning of the term *Christian*) will so fully appropriate the teaching of the cross and resurrection in their lives that they will be said to have the same mind that was in Christ Jesus. They will also do the works Jesus did, even as Jesus predicted. When faced with this sudden advent of a multitude of little Christs, the status quo will be powerless to stop it. Thus will the new age dawn.

Jesus was a prophet, and he saw this day coming from afar. That was why he did not despise the shame of the cross. He knew that the second coming Spirit incarnation of the new consciousness in the lives of many would be the result and fruition of his own life and work. Thus he was patient and long suffering about his own incarnation's seeming lack of success.

Spiritual consciousness development is actually a science, and when others in the scientific community begin to recognize it as such, as many of today's physicists are doing, it is a sure sign that its time has come. Before its time had fully come, the new consciousness was looked at as strictly a religious phenomenon, which meant that it was only for those who were religiously inclined. But the embracing of it as science is the proof that it is universal and enduring.

Jesus made the Christ known to human spiritual consciousness universally. Though men were not yet ready to embrace such a truth, he taught that the Christ Spirit was no respecter of persons. It was not therefore a matter of adhering to any particular religious tradition. Rather the Presence and substance of God in men would prove to be so expansive that it could bring all men to their knees in submission.

As human beings, the Christ Spirit has always been a part of our inner makeup, with its presence being realized in relation to our spiritual evolution. Thus there are no distinctions based on religion, race, or skin color. Scientifically, all human beings are capable of the same degree of spiritual consciousness evolution. Jesus not only taught God realization from a scientific universal angle, he gave us the most powerful key to the unlocking of this ultimate human potential. That key was the revelation of the redemptive nature of God.

It is the revelation of God's redemptive nature as given by Christ Jesus that has made us primed and ready for the next evolutionary step. True, it has taken time for this revelation to leaven human consciousness. But the full appropriation of any truth of this magnitude takes time.

The new consciousness may not be the ultimate evolutionary plateau for mankind. But one thing is certain: it is our *next* plateau. And before any higher planes can be realized, we must first thoroughly master that which is before us.

Progress in the human sphere will take place in leaps and bounds once the new consciousness is fully embraced. Individuals will know greater peace and fulfillment than ever before, and human society as a whole will be markedly transformed. Wars and regional hostilities will end; economic disparities will disappear, and disease will become a thing of the distant past. People will no longer be subjected to psychological conditioning at birth, but will be born free and innocent. Human culture will reflect the values of spiritual truth. The curse of Adam that has dominated this age of men will at long last be lifted.

Printed in the United States
By Bookmasters